OF MICE AND ME

by Michael B. Campbell

Copyright © 2017 by Michael B. Campbell, Prairie Moon Publilshing Inc. All rights reserved.

No part of this book may be reproduced or utilized in any form or by any means, electronic or mechanical, including photocopying, recording, or by information storage and retrieval system—except in the case of brief quotations embodied in critical articles and reviews—without permission from the publisher.

ISBN: 978-1-62660-130-7

Book design by MC Writing Services / Prairie Moon Publishing, Inc.
    301 South 50th Avenue
    Omaha NE 68132
    questions@mcwriting.com

OF MICE AND ME

THOUGHT DROPPINGS

MICHAEL B. CAMPBELL

FOR MY WIFE LAURA, OFTEN REFERRED TO
IN THIS BOOK AS MY GIRLFRIEND,
BECAUSE SHE DIDN'T AGREE TO MARRY ME
UNTIL AROUND CHAPTER "THE ORIENTEER."

SPECIAL THANKS TO MY SISTER CHERYL
FOR ACCIDENTALLY WRITING
THE "MOUSE POOP" CHAPTER FOR ME.

CONTENTS

LIFE LINES

In One Ear 3

Feeling Flushed 6

Hey There, Cowboy! 9

Springtime in Omaha 12

Cleaning Up 14

Just Skating By 17

Raising the Dead 22

Hail Mary 25

Pink Day 27

WHEN I WAS YOUR AGE

Finding My Direction 31

Back Door Boys 37

Cotton Candy: Into Thin Air 40

Birth Order 43

In the Real World 45

Poll Position 48

Kiddie Porn 50

Brain Pain 54

That's Snow Biz 58

The Funeral Procession 62

Model Behavior 67

A Moving Day 70

SOMETHING I ATE

- Trending Markets *79*
- Something Fishy. *82*
- You Are Where You Eat. *85*
- Party Time *89*
- We're Doomed. So What's for Dinner? . . . *92*
- Blow Me Away *95*
- Condimentary, My Dear Watson *98*
- The Boxer. *101*
- Don't Be Such a Square *104*
- Out of the Mold. *106*
- For Good Measure *109*

YOU ANIMAL

- Of Mice and Me. *113*
- Le Bark *117*
- Routine Maintenance *120*
- Pet Peeve *123*
- Paper Training *126*
- Mouse Poop. *128*

WHEELS

- Heck on Wheels. *135*
- Crunch Time *139*
- Driving Lessons. *142*
- Badass *145*
- A Bang-up Job *148*

Clutch Moment *151*
My Hot Car *156*
Going Down *160*

WHERE THE HEART IS

Special Delivery. *165*
Iced, Iced, Baby *170*
I'm with the Band *173*
The Orienteer *176*
In Stitches *178*
Naked Power *182*
In Your Dreams *186*
Go Fish *188*
Keys to Success *191*
What a Doll. *193*

IF YOU WANT MY ADVICE

Voting Signs. *197*
You Say You Want an Evolution. *200*
With Friends Like These *203*
Any Other Day *205*
A Night at the Opera *208*
Don't Call Me Rich *212*
Do It in Dubai *214*
Space-Age Technology. *217*
This Job Blows *221*
The iWish. *223*
Break a Leg *225*

ON HOLIDAY

A Year of Eating Dangerously 231

In the Bag 234

The Masked Pretender 237

Say It with Meat 240

Fire in the Fireplace 243

About the author 245

LIFE LINES

IN ONE EAR

Q-tips are the heroin of the hygiene world.

Sticking a Q-tip in your ear buzzes your synapses like being kissed on the back of the neck. Except being kissed on the back of the neck is perfectly good for you, as long as you are not being kissed by someone else's spouse.

A thing is usually bad for you if you can't stop yourself from moaning while you do it.

Q-tips don't clean your ear very well. I looked that up on the internet so I know what I'm talking about. They said you shouldn't remove cerumen from your ears. I think cerumen was one of the things the Wise Men gave baby Jesus. If a Wise Man pulled it out of his ear, he was probably just trying to make Jesus laugh, like when my Uncle Milton once pulled out a penny.

Removing the wax dries out your ear and makes it itch, so you grab for another Q-tip. Heroin, I tell you. Soon you're alone under a bridge with a box of dirty Q-tips in a brown paper bag, doing two at a time.

Q-tips mash down the tiny hairs inside your ear, so you end up with more dirt, more infections, and the most annoying affliction of all: people saying "I told you so."

When "ear candling" lit up as a fad, it claimed to remove ear wax by melting it with a candle stuck into the ear. It sounded to me like a fraternity dare. It didn't feel nearly as sexy as Q-tips, and after various people set their heads on fire and dripped hot wax onto their perforated eardrums, the fad blew out.

Dr. Rod Moser states that the safest tool for cleaning your ear is your elbow. Dr. Moser is as funny as my Uncle Milton.

The Chesebrough-Pond[1] company, makers of Q-tips, is very quiet on the subject because they know 99% of people buy Q-tips to stick in their ears. The company walks a delicate line: they cannot tell you not to stick a Q-tip in your ear because they'll go broke. But they can't *encourage* you to do it because when you drive one through your eardrum and into your brain, you'd sue, claiming it was all their idea. The packaging manages by saying Q-tips are *"the perfect tool for uses outside the ear."*

That's like saying heroin is the perfect drug for uses outside your veins. What uses are there, outside of the ear? Mouse barbells?

Their website doesn't offer any helpful tips, so to speak, probably because there aren't any. But I did learn the glorious history of Q-tips. They were invented by Leo Gerstenzang. Judging from his name I think he also invented the ricochet.

He started the Gerstenzang Infant Novelty Company, which was a pretty smart idea, since everything is a novelty to an infant. Originally called Baby Gays, the name was quickly changed to Q-tip, and sales improved. The Q standing for "quality," not as my mother would claim, "Quit sticking things in your ears." Doctors immediately declared Q-tips unsafe for sticking in your ears, an idea which hadn't occurred to anybody yet, and sales now surpass $400 million thanks to people doing what they're not supposed to. According to Wikipedia, uses include collecting DNA samples, applying makeup, establishing microbiological cultures on agar plates, hobby modeling,

---

1 Sounds like a place the Beatles would record an album.

measuring surface energy, and cleaning the laser of an optical drive. Most commonly, they are used for sticking in one's ear.

Medical Q-tips are made with wooden handles, because they'll withstand being sterilized in an autoclave. Plastic handled Q-tips would melt. Since I am not trusted with autoclaves, I get the plastic Q-tips.

To sum up the downside: sticking Q-tips in your ear has no medical benefit and poses risks including drying out the ear, packing wax painfully against your eardrum, perforating it altogether, and introducing bacteria, fungi, and insects.

The upside: they make you *purrrrr.*

FEELING FLUSHED

I got my water bill this week. My usage was five times higher than last year. It's the price I pay for not fixing the leaking toilet. At about $29 in parts plus a day's labor on my back under the bowl, it's a fair trade.

I know exactly how to fix a toilet. I know what's involved, because I've done it before. That's why I don't do it now.

The first time I peeled a toilet off the floor was when I remodeled the former Musette Bar. It had the kind of bathrooms you'd expect in a 70-year-old dive. I didn't want to enter the bathroom, much less lay down on the floor with a wrench and a flashlight, cheek to cheek with the toilet bowl, looking up from the bottom to remove the tank.

If you can find them under the sticky filth, the bolts will be rusted on. Urine is corrosive. It amazes me that a man can hit a tiny golf ball with a skinny club and knock it into a four-inch hole three hundred yards away, but he can't hit a foot-wide toilet bowl from thirty inches.

It's hard to drain all the water out of the tank and bowl before you remove them. Inevitably, it drips on your head. Yes, it's just water, the same water that comes out of the sink. But once it's been in the bowl, it's toilet water, and now it's running down your cheek.

Once the water tank is off, the toilet bowl peels away easily from the floor. The gooey connection that once existed between bowl and sewer pipe looks exactly like you'd expect, but it's not what you think. The gummy charcoal-colored goo is wax, once an amber-colored seal. It's fake shit, really, as real-looking as the fake vomit in the novelty store. It is Madame Tussaud mixed with Spencer Gifts.

It scrapes off easily enough with a putty knife. Nothing could look more repugnant, but to my surprise it doesn't stink that much. Of all the vile places to find yourself, standing over an open sewer pipe isn't so bad. Good news, but not so good you look forward to it.

One of my tenants, Jimmy, lived in a humble apartment above the bar. A one-eyed Marine veteran and retired union bricklayer, Jimmy's job was to defend his stool[2] at the R Bar down the street from 3 PM until close. He gave the bar owner his disability check at the beginning of each month, and it was meted out across thirty days to pay Jimmy's tab so he didn't spend it all in one night. It was an arrangement of convenience and necessity.

Jimmy didn't walk well sober. Weaving home very drunk late one night, he managed to conquer the long, pulsing stairway, making it to the bathroom just in time to relieve himself, at which point he got the spins. The small bathroom became a white-tiled carousel. He grabbed the metal medicine cabinet to steady himself, but it broke loose from the wall, smashing open the ceramic toilet tank on the way down.

At 6 AM the next morning, when Jimmy didn't show up for their standing coffee date in his kitchen, neighbor George checked in on him. Neither was in the best of health, and they were otherwise so routine that George had begun to worry. George knew Jimmy had gotten up because he could hear the water was running. He found Jimmy asleep on the wet floor, medicine cabinet clutched to his chest like a teddy bear. The toilet, trying to fill a tank that no longer had walls, was now raining onto the bar a floor below. The new perfor-

---

2 Given the context of this story, I need to clarify that I mean "chair" this time.

mance stage I had finished building just the day before was now curled up like a potato chip.

I had to replace my third toilet.

Less than a year later, Jimmy didn't conquer the long stairway. George came home to find him two-thirds of the way up, face down dead. Jimmy had lived there on and off since 1950, and the building didn't feel complete without him. We mourned. The R Bar forgave his tab.

Reattaching a toilet is a snap. Place a fresh new golden wax seal over the sewer pipe, align the bowl on top of it, sit on it to smoosh the wax down, screw it down with fresh, shiny new bolts (stainless steel that won't rust!), secure the water tank above the bowl, attach the water connections, turn on the water, scream because water is flying everywhere, shut the water back off, tighten the connections, and — *voilà!* — you're done. Okay, not *voilà*. *Voilà* is not a toilet word.

After replacing your first toilet, you can't wash your hands enough. I took a whole shower, scrubbing with an abrasive, long-handled brush because I didn't want to touch myself. Some sweet-smelling lotion afterwards, nice white clothes. Fresh garden tomato bruschetta, a glass of red wine. A spirited discussion of live theatre with my sweetheart. Anything to make me feel I was back to civilization.

I wonder what red wine the plumber recommends?

HEY THERE, COWBOY!

What do you do when you find out your best friend has been keeping the biggest, juiciest secret from you for years? Why hadn't he ever told me? It's not like I'd publish his private story in a book or anything.

After a long struggle to sell a failing bar, I planned a long weekend visit to Portland, Oregon. My friend TJ had built himself a little Eden on a secluded mountainside. I hoped it would be a rinse retreat, to help put one life behind me and orient my heart toward a new one. The bar sale was delayed. I already had my tickets so I went anyway. Instead of a philosophical retreat, we just drank margaritas all weekend.

Back in junior high, TJ and I would hole up in his bedroom and play guitars. We'd put on an LP and sit at the altar of his fancy stereo system, studying what the artist was up to, trying to imitate it. TJ would sag into his squeaky beanbag chair and I'd lean my back up against the side of his bed as we strummed through John Denver, Loggins & Messina and the Doobie Brothers. This was before they invented gangs.

TJ builds guitars now, the most beautiful instruments I've ever seen. While I was there he let me help work on one. I got to play about $50,000 worth of other people's guitars in between rounds of pool, margaritas and his outdoor hot tub.

At the end of my first day there, I was deliriously relaxed and sated. My bleary, lime-tinted eyes grew heavy. I was ready for bed.

"Did you give him the cowboy sheets?" his girlfriend asked.

"They're already in the guest room."

"Cowboy sheets?" I blinked awake. I feared sheets used by another visitor who smelled of cattle and chewing tobacco.

"I found TJ a set of flannel sheets with cowboys on them," she explained, as if that explained anything. She's a master shopper. She could find weapons-grade plutonium for 30% off. "They're magic sheets. You'll sleep great."

"Cowboy sheets?" I repeated.

"Since I was a kid I wanted cowboy sheets," TJ told me. "Mom asked me what kind of sheets I wanted, and I told her cowboy sheets. She went to Sears, but she came back with the wrong sheets."

"Well?" I waited. "What did she come back with?"

He gave me a steely look. "She brought back the wrong thing. I begged her to go back and exchange them for cowboy sheets. *Begged*," he repeated, as a desperate schoolboy look returned to his eyes. "She said returning them would be too much trouble. 'But Mom,' I said, 'you *work there!*' But she wouldn't do it. She never did."

"Seriously — what were you stuck with?"

A pained look curtained his face.

"Cinderella."

TJ is funny. Having gone through junior and senior high with him, I've had pretty much every drink come out my nose, so this margarita was just one more.

"Cinderella *sheets?*" I snorted.

"Yep. Little Cinderellas all over."

"So what did you do? Just use plain white sheets?"

"I only had the one set. We'd take them off, wash them, put them back on."

"The Cinderella sheets?"

"Yes."

"You mean to tell me that when I was in your room…"

"Yes."

"…leaning on your bed…"

"Yes."

"…you had Cinderella sheets, *at that time,* on your bed?"

"Under the bedspread."[3]

Years ago I took karate lessons. I earned a black belt, and even became an instructor for a while. TJ had been *my* instructor. He owned the school. Because I was as big as he was, he liked to use me for demonstrations. During one, he picked me up and held me over his head like a giant letter *T,* pausing casually mid-throw to explain the technique to the other students before I was tossed to the floor like bag of sand. Another night he knocked me out cold with a heel to my temple. My head has been on the receiving end of many fists, but at six-foot two-inches tall, it doesn't encounter many feet. TJ gets a certain blank look in his eye before he pummels you. I know that look very well. He had that look now.

Dumfounded, I said, "I cannot believe, for all these years, that I never knew you slept in Cinderella sheets."

He didn't reply, just continued giving me that look. I can't believe he'd think I'd tell anybody.

---

[3] Parents: this is how you get your child to make his bed every day.

SPRINGTIME IN OMAHA

The sights and smells of springtime in Omaha have returned like sandhill cranes to fill my Midwestern senses with the comforting assurance that the cycle of life is ever spinning.

A daisy-yellow backhoe, it's lanky elbow lifting with a flamingo's grace, picks up fat chunks of my street and feeds them into the upturned belly of stained dump truck, the way a robin feeds puke to her young.

Tanned, fit men in hard, yellow bonnets scurry to and fro like picnic ants, with dirt in their shovels to build brown hills over here from dirt they carted away from over there. They sow rows of sewer pipe to carry away the fresh spring rains and toilet flushings, hidden veins throbbing under the thin skin of our city.

The trees, grass and cars are dressed in the silver-gray gossamer dust exhaled by giant circular saws squawking and pecking brand new cement into squares as neat as Grandmother's brownies.

My winter routine is freshened by surprising new sights as traffic cones detour me, along with a flood of other drivers, away from the steaming, oily new asphalt of busy Leavenworth Street into the intimate neighborhood avenues filled with darting children and bicycles.

OF MICE AND ME

I welcome the migration of the College World Series baseball tourists, who signal a left turn, then turn right from the center lane. Like an intricate mating dance, they execute their native Texan 12-point parallel parking, coming to a satisfied rest with one wheel perched on the curb. Their chicks hatch from the SUV, resplendent in bright orange plumage, cargo shorts and flip-flop sandals on their white feet as they flip-flop across our sunny city, waddling into our elegant restaurants, unaware of the local custom of removing one's hat.

Free outdoor concerts and art festivals blossom, where we gather thick as pigeons on a field-sized quilt of sun-bleached blankets and blue plastic tarps joined end-to-end to protect us from the young green grass.

It is God's grace that the furious winter past is now only a nebulous memory. For this one season we let ourselves forget that, as sure as the Earth spins, winter will return with a fresh layer of wet gray snow, and the following spring will freeze and thaw today's new cement into manageable chunks chewed by God's molars into to gravel under the black heels of trucks carrying bread and beer and furniture, leaving behind yawning potholes, the natural predator of the beepy Smart car. But just as certain, the men in their yellow bonnets and trucks and cranes will return too, as the spring cycle of Omaha blossoms all over again.

CLEANING UP

It's getting harder to buy soap. Maybe it's a guy thing, but once I find a laundry soap that works, I stop comparing brands. I go to the store and buy my soap, ignoring all the brightly-colored, orchid-scented, double-concentrated, softener-added products surrounding it.

I made my choice a long time ago. My daughter did a little research project in high school and found that one brand of laundry soap actually cleaned a little better, and since I didn't have an opinion of my own, I bought that one and have used it ever since. One thing my daughter and I agree on is that she is usually right.

Luckily my options are few. Because I use a front-loading machine, I have to use "high-efficiency" detergent. Apparently regular-efficiency soap will bubble up into a cumulonimbus cloud. Maybe "high-efficiency" is badly named, since it bubbles less. But the bottom line is that there are only a handful of H.E. choices.

Calamity struck. One day my detergent was gone from the store shelves, replaced with "For Sensitive Skin, No Perfumes or Dyes!" My first thought was *why you gotta go and change everything?* My second thought was *what's this — you were poisoning me this whole time?* My third: *Those chemicals that irritate sensitive skin (apparently not my leathery ass) are probably the same chemicals I trust to get the mustard stains off my shirt.*

I bought it anyway. I hid my face at the check-out, feeling like a sensitive-skinned sissy.

I know using the righ kind of soap is important. I learned the lesson from my dishwasher, on a day I ran out of dishwasher soap. I was on my way out the door, leaving the country,[4] and I didn't want the dirty dishes in my dishwasher to evolve into a thriving, self-governing community before my return. All I had was regular liquid dish soap, the blue kind you use in the sink. "How different can it be?" I squirted some into the little door cup of the dishwasher, shut the door and hit "Go." Then I went.

As I grabbed my last suitcase and headed out the door, something caught my eye — something much like the oozing protagonist in *The Blob*, only whiter. Right before my eyes it silently obscured the wooden kitchen floor with three inches of foam, oozing out of the dishwasher door seams like cotton candy.

I shut off the dishwasher and gingerly opened the door. I grabbed a dustpan and began shoveling foam into the sink, which filled after about four scoops.

It is nearly impossible to get bubbles to go down a drain. They float happily above their eminent doom, and all the hand-corralling, swatting and cuss words won't make them obey gravity.

On the plus side, my kitchen floor has never been cleaner.

I had a similar adventure after spilling a jar of instant coffee on the floor.[5] Using a wet mop to clean instant coffee just makes a pot of coffee on the floor. The more I mopped, the more coffee I made. I'm impressed how much coffee they can squeeze into those little brown crystals. Go science.

---

4 Willingly.
5 I had to choose between sharing this story and admitting I ever used instant coffee.

Ironically, you have to clean up soap. Seems like soap ought to be self-cleaning, but I hire a cleaning lady twice a month to get "soap scum" off my shower. When you buy it, it's soap, but when you use it it turns to scum, and not the scum you were using it on. So what does she use to clean soap scum? Soap. It's job security.

My grapefruit-scented face soap comes in a little pump bottle. (Some girl convinced me that using a bar of Lava on my face was not good.) It's a nice little bottle, a shame to throw away, so I thought I'd keep it around for, um, something. I was feeling recycle-y. I rinsed the remnant soap out, which bubbled and bubbled out the top. I rinsed. It bubbled. A-n-d b-u-b-b-l-e-d. About twenty gallons of hot water and a size-14 carbon footprint later, I gave up and threw the bottle away.

I can be a Luddite but I don't yearn for the days where we[6] cleaned our clothes by banging them onto rocks. Yet as I encounter about fifty varieties of soap each day: body soap, shampoo, toothpaste, face soap, dish soap, dish*washer* soap, laundry soap, carwash soap and all manner of solvents I have in my workshop, I gotta think somebody out there is really cleaning up.

---

6 Who am I kidding? By "we," I mean women.

JUST SKATING BY

My first rollerskates were hand-me-downs, with a metal frame that clamped to your shoe by adjusting its length and locking it with a key. Skinny steel wheels with steel bearings ground their way over the gritty concrete, and I felt every pebble. Eventually I dismantled the two halves, screwed them on opposite ends of a piece of wood and made my first skateboard.

I visited a roller rink for the first time in 1972. They rented fancy skates with high-top shoes and fat plastic wheels. Still, I wasn't good at it. I felt like a colt with lead hooves. I fell a lot. A fat kid ran over my finger. It seemed like everyone else was a gazelle, spinning tricks in the center of the circle like Peggy Fleming, while I clomped around the perimeter, clinging to the rail.

When the in-line Rollerblade craze rolled through the '90s, a friend and I dove in like fiends. We got good. We skated hard, invented cool tricks, argued over the ideal wheel hardness and best bearing lube. We geeked. And like most things geeky, it ran its course. I haven't looked inside my smelly skate bag in years, except to reminisce.

So when a gang of friends invited me recently to join them for Adults Only Night at Skate Daze, after we had stuffed ourselves with pizza and beer at a birthday party, I rubbed that finger as I said, "Yeah, sure." I added without conviction, "Sounds like fun."

Maybe it would be. I never really gave those traditional 4-wheel skates another try. I prefer to be brilliant, and if I'm not brilliant at something right away I usually give up on it.

I entered Skate Daze warily. I didn't see a rink, just a gymnasium full of old video games: *Defender, Galaga,* and various car-racing games with pixelly graphics, vintage Atari. I slowed as I tried to make sense of a shooting game titled *Cops vs. the Japs.* I ran a finger across the dusty Air Hockey table as one would admire a restored 1959 Eldorado. This place didn't feel retro, just old.

I worked my way through the game room and around the corner to find the skating rink. The skaters hadn't changed much either. Granted, it was Adults Only Night, which sounds sexy but isn't. This is where people hang out after A.A. meetings. It was ringed with the serious faces of serious skaters. The rental clerk was as bored and cynical as ever.

But what's this? Along with 4-wheel skates, one could rent in-line skates now — something forbidden in the '70s.

This changed everything! My confidence grew. Maybe this would work out after all. I grabbed a pair and headed for a bench.

"In-lines?" a passing friend commented as I laced them up. "Do your parents know you're gay?"

I hadn't set foot in the rink yet and already felt like I had failed something. "What's wrong with in-lines?"

"Nothinnngg…" she giggled as she sashayed away.

It brought back a conversation at a bar a few months back, when I learned that a friend still owned a pair of rollerblades. He's an athletic guy and I knew I could hold my own, so I said, "We should go skate."

"Really? You're going to go rollerblading together?" his girlfriend commented, eyebrows fully raised. "Are you going to wear tight little cut-offs and hold hands?"

It caught me off-guard. Something very suggestive and very public must have happened on rollerblades between my heyday and now. A David Bowie video on MTV, maybe? I can be counted on to be clueless about pop culture.

Call me gay all you want. After my divorce in the late '80s I moved into an apartment tower, and after saying "hi" every day to the nice lady at the front desk where I picked up my mail, I asked if she'd like to join me for lunch. "Uh, okay," she said, hesitating. "I thought you were gay."

"Why? What makes you think that?"

She gave it a moment's thought. "You have good manners. You dress nice."

I felt a little thrill at that. No one had ever accused me of dressing nice before. She added, "And you live here."

That part made sense. The apartment tower was downtown in an urban, very gay-welcoming building.

Later I was thrilled to be invited to a neighbor's apartment, a local media power couple hosting a party right down the hall. He was a copywriter, she was a popular news anchor. The gathering was full of local celebrities, and I tried not to look too star-struck as one of my favorite radio personalites chatted with me over appetizers. It was an exciting evening and I left elated, but when I encountered the hostess the next morning in the elevator, she wouldn't even look at me. Her husband later explained (also in the elevator) that his wife had invited me in hopes of fixing me up with big-shot radio guy, whom we all knew was gay, and who was a bit embarrassed to discover I wasn't. She was mortified. And sure enough, I never got another invitation.

When people get divorced they often try on a new skin to help them face their new life. Some men grow beards. I bought new clothes. To have people think I was gay at that point in my life felt nice, one more mask over my torn-up life, something to make the past feel more past.

So what was the problem, then? Why did those comments make me feel like I was in junior high again?

"Because you felt ostracized," a friend explained. "Excluded. *Reduced.* Pretty much what gay men feel when they hear it said that way."

It was time. Amid the thumping of Metallica and swirling disco ball sparkles I clomped my way across the carpet and stepped gingerly onto the wood rink with its swirling drain of skaters, keeping myself within an arm's length of the side wall. *Fit-fit-fit-fit!* Four skaters brushed by, racing in perfect lock-step, and I felt their wind as they flew by like bats. They were resplendent in tattoos and piercings, heads shaved, and as if to double-down on their rebelliousness, their old-school 4-wheel skates were unlaced. No Hell's Angels, but pretty tough.

They followed tight behind their leader, matching his every slouchy move, flannel shirts trailing like Superman capes. Each followed so close behind the next they were touching crotch to butt, in a line like they were racing in the Tour du France.

"Shadow-skating," a companion commented as she watched admiringly. "That is so bad-ass!" At that moment the DJ, dressed in a referee shirt, cued up *Careless Whisper* by George Michael, once famous for his tight little cut-offs.

Skate Daze had become a portal into role-reversal, an Upside-down Land for stereotypes.

"That guy is flirting with me," my friend mused. "Whenever he passes me he does an extra little dance move."

"Like a mating dance?"

"Yeah," she said. "Skate-and-mate."

I looked up. All the women were skating limply in circles, minding their own business. The guys were undulating like temptresses. Mr. Skate-and-Mate fluttered by again, backwards and doing cross-overs, as he grinned at my friend.

"Wow," I said, "you're skater bait."

I'm never gonna dance again
The way I danced with you-hoo...

The skater dudes were peacocks on wheels, a frenzy of flourish. Not one pair of in-lines on the whole rink but mine. I felt like I was in court, arguing my case in my head. *But I rented these skates here! From you! These are your skates!*

One of my friends skated by, arms at his side, enjoying a nice time, blissfully alone in his happy thoughts, enviably unpretentious. He actually *is* gay.

"Couples Skate!" the referee announced. The lights dimmed, leaving the lone disco ball to scatter disorienting white stars across the floor. In the past I always had to leave the floor during Couples Skate, always making an effort to look like I coincidentally had something else to do. I said goodbye to Skater Bait and jumped onto the rink.

By then I had found my skate legs. I pushed hard and gathered speed until I caught up with my girlfriend, who was practicing her Gloria Gaynor disco moves.

I tried to skate backwards past her and shine my best Ricardo Montalban grin, but my skates tangled like bumper cars and I settled for facing forward, grasping her hand. An older couple floated by, poised in ballroom position. They rotated as a pair, precise as a music box.

"Now *that*," I said, "is bad-ass."

RAISING THE DEAD

Last night I slept like the dead. Unlike the dead, I woke up feeling great. So I guess I slept more like Jesus. I didn't sleep like a baby. When I owned a bar I slept like a baby, waking up screaming every three hours.

I shared that notion with some friends, and one suggested that I probably slept more like Lazarus. I suppose it was asking too much of my friends to think I might do anything like Jesus.

As close as I ever got to being like Jesus was when I wore a scruffy beard and my curly hair long, draping myself in flowing linen shirts and huarache sandals.[7] It is a common fashion of newly divorced men.

In church one morning a little girl looked up at me in awe and asked, "Are you Jesus?"

If she would have said "George Carlin" I would have teased her by pretending I was, but I don't mess with Jesus and I personally know three friends who have been struck by lightning. Clouds gathered over my head while a clear voice inside me advised, "Don't *even*."

"No, little angel," I smiled. "I'm Michael. But Jesus thinks you're a wonderful little girl and He told me to tell you hi."

I once had a dream about Jesus. In my dream He wore the exact drapy linen you'd expect, but He lived in an enormous sand castle.

---

[7] I used to buy them three pairs at a time in case they became unavailable. I just checked, and they've been available since World War II.

Along with a few other sychophants I followed Him up a long, narrow stairway within the walls. Eventually we came to a tiny balcony where we peered out upon throngs of people far below, going about their business like proverbial ants.[8] There was room on the ledge for only three of us at a time, and when it was my turn to look, I wedged myself into the opening at His left. Just then the small sandcastle ledge began to soften, to sag, then to collapse beneath my feet. I was blocked from retreating by the people crowded up behind me, and I began to slip away. It was a long way down and I panicked, yet at the same time I was embarrassed to be enduring this indignity right in front of Jesus. Without looking, Jesus touched my chest with the back of His hand, suspended my fall and set me back on solid ground. There was no cheer or clapping. I don't think anyone else noticed, or if they did it was just one more ho-hum miracle.

So I didn't sleep like Lazarus either. Lazarus, according to the New Testament, went to bed gravely ill. He sent for his friend Jesus to visit him. Jesus, hearing the news while glad-handing in another town, promised He'd go, but dawdled amid the crush of admirers. By the time He finally arrived at the home of Lazarus, He was harshly informed by the poor man's shrill wife that Lazarus had been dead in his tomb for four days, and *who do you think you are, Mr. Big Shot? You think you're too important to visit your dying friend? For shame!*

Jesus did what any man does under such a blistering attack: He denied everything. "Dead? Nobody's dead," Jesus shrugged innocently. "Lazarus isn't dead." It's not cool to argue with Jesus, but nonetheless they rolled away the stone for a peek. Out stumbled a bleary, shroud-wrapped Lazarus, feeling his way out of the cave into the blinding sunlight to many *ooohs* and *ahhhs*. Neat trick, Jesus.

---

8 Actually, according to the written record, Jesus did not offer any proverbs about ants.

My mind reels at all the trouble I could have avoided if I could have changed the circumstances after the fact. "I didn't forget your anniversary, honey! Look — *[pling!]* our anniversary is *tomorrow!*"

Of all the miracles Jesus performed — healing the sick, feeding the hordes, water to wine — this seems to be the only stunt He pulled to get himself out of a tight spot. Yes, He walked on water, but that was to prove a point. He didn't jump out of the storm-swamped boat to escape an angry woman. After He gave his friends a good scare and gave a little speech, He stepped back into the boat.

You could argue that He blew life back into Lazarus to impress the onlooking Jews, many of whom converted on the spot. But they would have been just as impressed — maybe more so — if Jesus had turned the shrieking woman into a pillar of salt. Oldie, but goodie.

Jesus was risen. Lazarus was awakened. After sleeping like the dead, I was alone.

One detail about my dream I left out: Jesus was a woman. After She saved me from falling off the ledge, She gave me a gentle kiss. It was the sweetest, kindest, most grace-filled kiss I could dream up. I woke from the dream and wrote it all down, and while I usually don't remember my dreams at all, I recall this one vividly. I know there are those who will want to tar and feather me for suggesting such a thing, even though it was just in a dream. I delayed this confession so that, if you're warming up your tar, I could still get the rest of the story out first.

HAIL MARY

I gazed out my window like I always do when I'm trying to do anything but work, and the Virgin Mary appeared in my driveway. I guess she didn't exactly *appear* — I just noticed her face in the coloration of the concrete. Plain as day, sober as an undertaker.

I looked away. I looked back. Yep, still there.

My first thought was: "Rich! I'm *rich!*" I imagined a long line of devotees paying me a dollar a peek. I could set up a lemonade stand. Then just thinking about all those people poking about my backyard made me question the blessing of it all.

I looked again. She still looked like Mary, but maybe a bit more like one of the cast of *Cats,* unless Mary has whiskers, which she very well might — you know they always airbrush that stuff out for the portraits. The lyric "Not a sound from the pavement" occurred to me. There are a lot of Andrew Lloyd Weber fans out there, but I'm not sure they'd make the pilgrimage to Omaha to see a Holy Cats apparition. My stock was dropping.

So how does one know for sure that it's a *sign?* When Mary appeared as a grilled cheese sandwich to Diana Duyser a few years ago, the Golden Palace Casino bought it for $28,000. How did they know they had the real thing? I saw it and thought Mary looked suspiciously like a Ziegfeld Girl. Besides, the sandwich had a bite taken out of it. Doesn't that lower its value? Who wants a half-eaten Virgin Mary?

They have this going for them: if you google "Virgin Mary images," a lot of grilled cheese sandwiches turn up.

Why would Mary appear in my driveway? All I can come up with is this: concrete is 80% sand, and so is the Promised Land.

What should I do when it snows? I can't leave her like that, but I don't feel right shoveling her face. I'm already parking on the other side of the driveway, just to be safe.

I'd show you a picture, but like a vampire her face doesn't turn up in photo searches. Maybe that's some kind of supernatural rule. I suppose when it comes to trademark infringement, Catholics don't mess around.

As I write this, my enthusiasm for the whole thing is fading. The face is starting to look more like Chandler from *Friends*. The only entertainment value left is the curiosity of seeing who appears next. MC Hammer? It's a parade of has-beens, a driveway episode of *The Love Boat*.

[sigh.]

I still don't feel like working. A grilled cheese sandwich sounds good right now.

PINK DAY

Happy Pink Day!

Pink Day is not on the calendar. Its celebration depends entirely on the weather. The first sunny, warm day in spring, after the snow has melted and grass starts prying itself up from being face down in the mud, is Pink Day.

Tree branches swell with horny buds. Cardinals and robins sing dirty songs to the opposite sex. Humans doff their shirts and shoes and offer up their pale pink skin to the pagan sun of spring.

Pink skin in July looks unhealthy, but in March in the Midwest it is as natural and beautiful as a mother robin puking worms into her baby's eager mouth.

I donned a thick sweater and a corduroy shirt and managed to have lunch out on the patio. I felt like an antenna, sucking up the sun's energy as it recharged my near-dead batteries. I drew a deep breath of Pink Day air. It smells less of sprouting daffodils than of thawing dog poop.

My dog is rewarded with a little biscuit after he poops outside. Pretty much all he eats are those biscuits, so that's what his poop consists of. His little Shih Tzu turds come out like macadamia nuts, exactly the size of those treats. If I could get him to eat his own poop he could be self-rewarding. In spring, my yard smells of wet Milk Bones.

The lawn service guy just spread a spring layer of organic fertilizer. It smells like corn flakes. He says it comes from chickens. I don't know if he means chicken droppings, or chicken feed, or, well, *chickens*. But it's clear how much they rely on corn for chicken feed.

As I exhale that deep lungful of corn flakes and poopcicles, I hear the sweet, optimistic sound of a cardinal calling for his mate. His song is drowned out by a passing motorcycle. It must be fun to ride a Harley. In high school, I myself proudly earned a citation for disturbing the peace, thanks to my bike's after-market muffler. But I'm not on a motorcycle now, so the noise isn't fun. I respond with a bird of my own, and loudly sing my song of spring entitled, *Shut The Fuck Up You Self-Centered Jackass on a Harley*.[9]

After I finish this essay I'm going to celebrate Pink Day with tastes of summer weather: a margarita, maybe some corn chips. I'll sit on my front porch and wave as my pink neighbors parade by, friendly flamingos of spring.

---

9 It's a real song. I'm still polishing up the lyrics.

WHEN I WAS YOUR AGE

FINDING MY DIRECTION

Some people have perfect pitch. A person with perfect pitch can hear a note and tell you it's an F-sharp, or B-flat, or whatever. Generally, I avoid such people at parties because they understand something I don't. Same with accountants.

Most of us have *relative* pitch. I can sing *Do-Re-Mi* in such a way that you'll recognize the song right away, but my notes might not be the same pitch as the notes you would have started on, and both of us may be a few notes away from what's on the sheet music.

A few of us are just plain tone-deaf and bray like goats, which is fine too because goats are cute.

With relative pitch you can sing *Happy Birthday* along with other people just fine. You may find yourself straining halfway through the song because the person who started the *Haaaaaappy...* picked a note way higher than you were ready for, but who knew? Same problem with *The Star-Spangled Banner*: you can tell from four bars away that you started too high and now have no chance of hitting that *rockets red glaaare* part in the middle without yodeling. But really, who cares?

The guy with perfect pitch, that's who. Two notes into the song his ears start ringing like a grammar school fire alarm and he'll blurt out,

"Stop stop *stop!* That's not what key it's in. *Wrong key!*" After such an outburst, the party is pretty much over.

Happy Birthday was written[10] in the key of G, which means it starts on a D note. (Don't ask.) People with perfect pitch can sing a D note on command. That sounds like a lovely talent, but the flip side is that every time someone sings *Happy Birthday* in a different key, which is to say every time, it sounds wrong to them. Out of envy I would hate people with perfect pitch, except that God has already smitten them ahead of me.

I've played guitar since I was a kid. I can tune one up in seconds. It'll sound fine, unless you play it next to another guitar that has been tuned to correct pitch. Mine might be a whole note lower or higher, because the note to which I matched all the others was off in the first place. Thanks, relative pitch.

To get around this shortcoming, I have various strategies for tuning accurately:

- Play in front of someone who has perfect pitch, and see if they wince.
- Pick up a phone. Almost all land-line dial tones are an F note. Match the F on my guitar to it. The hardest part is finding a land-line phone.
- Use a tuning fork. It's fun and cool. I keep one in my case.

To use a tuning fork, whack it. It vibrates with the faintest hum, almost a whisper. You can barely hear it, because there's nothing for it to resonate against. But touch the ball end to the wood of a guitar

---

10 Yes, Happy Birthday was "written," mostly by sisters Patty and Mildred Hill. Warner Music Group/Chappell Music owned the copyright through the year 2030. That means every time you sang Happy Birthday publicly, you legally owed them a royalty. At last report, this earned Warner $5000 per day. In 2015 a judge ruled the copyright invalid. Party-poopers.

and the whole instrument will sing the tuning fork's note. Likewise, a friend showed me that you can press the end of the ringing tuning fork against your front tooth and your whole skull will resonate a perfect A-440. Nobody else hears a thing. This is a fun party trick if you don't mind a tuning fork that has touched everyone's teeth.

Sure, I could use an electronic guitar tuner, but where's the art in that? Using a guitar tuner is like filling out a crossword puzzle from the answer sheet.

Like my relative pitch, I have relative map skills. I can read and understand a map perfectly well regardless of which way it is pointing. This means I'll always turn right if I am supposed to turn right. However, I may turn north when I'm supposed to go south.

Worse, in the real world I have a perfect sense of direction, but a backwards sense of where everything actually *is*. This was the fault of my 4th grade teacher. While we learned map skills, my desk faced south, which is to say backwards. As I learned the names, shapes and locations of every state in the U.S., I was facing exactly the wrong way. Ask me to point north, and I'll point north every time. Ask me to point to California, and I'll point to New York.

Experts say language is best learned before the age of three. Map skills are best learned by age nine, after which the sense of place becomes cast in bone. As a result, I am doomed to forever see the world upside down.

Right now I'm looking out my window at Farnam Street, and I know I'm looking east. I know that beyond a few hills and past one river lies Iowa, because I've been over there. Beyond that, my brain starts expecting Wyoming, Idaho and Oregon. I've been to those states too, but I flew there on a plane so I didn't really learn anything. Flying in a plane is like riding an elevator: the door closes, then reopens to a completely different place, with no real appreciation of how you got there.

Here's what I have to do to actually find something: point to where I think it is, freeze my body in that position, and then rotate myself 180 degrees. It's like having perfect un-pitch. Anti-pitch.

I suppose I could do what the pioneers did: cross the United States on foot, step by step, mile by mile, experiencing the sights, smells and spirit of every hill in the whole continent. I find it's easier to just be wrong.

In that 4th grade class one morning, the teacher pulled down a wall-sized map of the Western Hemisphere like a huge windowshade, and turned to her eager students. "Who can point out the United States?" Every hand went up except one.

Every class has one hard-luck kid. He just wants the day to be over. He keeps his head down, hoping not to be picked on as the rest of us battle to position ourselves into the hierarchy of life. In this class, it was Earl, and the teacher said the one word he dreaded.

"Earl?"

There was a short pause, then he rose reluctantly from his chair in the back of the classroom. There's no hurry when you're walking to the gallows. Everyone rotated in their chairs to watch him shuffle down the aisle, like a reluctant bride.

As Earl passed midway down the center of the classroom, the laces of his large, untied tennis shoes tangled. He tripped, sprawling face-down in a rumpled thud.

We roared. Hyenas. Jackals. Crows.

He picked himself up and resumed his death march towards the map. He ran his finger across the brightly colored shapes, hoping one might reach out to save him. He was somewhere over Tibet.

The teacher, aptly named Fairchild, tried not to blink. She had hoped to toss him an easy softball, not this grenade. After an eternal twenty seconds she asked, "Can anyone help Earl?" Every hand shot up. All of us could point out the United States. None of us helped Earl.

We looked forward to recess He dreaded it.

The next day, after she arranged to have him out of the room, Mrs. Fairchild told us Earl's story. She had visited the dark home of his parents, who were both congenitally deaf. He wasn't read to as a kid. No bedtime stories. Everything in school was as unfamiliar to him as the Moon. Tears pushed their way to her eyes and her voice began to warble as she told us his story. We watched in stunned silence. Many of us had never seen an adult cry before, certainly never a teacher. It's like seeing your teacher grocery shopping. You think, are they allowed to *do* that?

After that year I never saw Earl again. A few of the kids stood up for him on the playground, but many of us were reluctant to give up the lazy joy of feeling superior.

In junior high I began hanging out with my friend-for-life, TJ. We played guitars in his basement, singing along to his record player. I noticed that whenever the song moved to a new chord, TJ dropped whatever syllable he was singing, as if his entire brain was required by his fingers to find the next chord:

> *Hello darkness, my old*
> *— end, I've come to talk with you*
> *— ennn, because a vision softly*
> *— eeeping left its seeds while I was*
> *— eeping, and the — sion that was — ted in*
> *my — ain...*

Of course I teased him. I was a junior high boy, and teasing was my trade. I made fun of him, and as easy as flicking off a light switch he never sang in public again. Ever.

He had a nice voice. I silenced it.

All these years later, I still write songs and perform on stages large and small. I'm grateful to have a decent sense of pitch, and a gift for picking out harmony. I'm sensitive to music. It sings directly to my soul and plays itself in my mind all day like a radio. It's part of my identity, which is why it's so hard for me to understand how my heart could have been so tone-deaf.

BACK DOOR BOYS

"You will *not* eat *that* in *this* house."

I froze in place, my finger still tucked under the sardine can's opener key. I looked up at Mom. I looked down at the can, as if to verify that *that* was what she meant. I looked back up at Mom.

"It's okay, Mom — it's food," I replied hopefully.

"I *know* what it *is*. You'll spill it. Sardines stink. You'll stink up the whole stinking house and the stink will never stop stinking. We will not live in a house that stinks."

She was right. Earlier that summer while swimming at a lake I got hit in the mouth by a bluegill and the oily taste didn't leave my lips for days. Sardines are worse. Still, I was crestfallen.

Dad was undeterred. He took the tin out of my hand, tucked a sleeve of Zesta saltines under his arm and grabbed a fork. "Outside, Moose.[11] Back porch."

Dad built the back porch a few years earlier. The original puny cement steps were now invisible underneath a roomy four-foot square of sturdy, handsome redwood. I liked sitting on its long steps, as strong and reassuring as my father. Each step was just the right height, I thought, as I wrapped my arms around my gangly knees and reeled my red Keds in tight. Dad's legs arched over two steps.

---

[11] He did not call me "Moose" because I was big and strong. Here is Dad math: Michael → Mickey → Mickey Mouse → Mickey Moose → Moose.

Dad was a conservative eater at the dinner table, but there were a few bolder foods which delivered him to a drooling delirium. Rocky Mountain oysters. Real oysters. Sardines.

Occasionally he'd bring home a tin of sardines packed in oil or mustard — my favorite! — and scan the room with a grin of "who's with me?" He used to enlist one of my older brothers or sisters, but they were all beyond that now. I got the nod. "Back porch, Moose." Just Dad and me, just the way I liked it.

He let me open the sardine tin. That was an honor I executed with great ceremony. Each can came with a key used to peel off the cover and roll it down like sheets off a bed. The inside of the can glistened green and copper, precious oil dripping back onto the neatly stacked fishes inside.

These sardines were perfect. Uniform. Identical. This bunch still had their heads — sometimes they don't — and the eyes looked up at nothing, a row of stoic soldiers before their king.

With a toss of his palm, Dad let me go first. I broke into the shiny perfection, lifting the first sardine out gingerly, trying not to break its soft body or tear the delicate skin.

I once bit a sardine in half so I could peer inside, to see the guts and bones, perplexed that it all tasted and felt just like the flesh. But it was better not to look. I didn't want my uneasiness to show.

I carefully laid the slick morsel across its cracker bed, diagonally like Dad taught me, handling it as carefully as nitroglycerine, Mom's warning still in my ear.

The whole sardine was smaller than my pinky. I ate it in one bite: the tiny head, the black eyes, the limp fins, the soft bones. It released a spurt of oil and spice.

We didn't talk. I was aware of the quiet crunch of saltine, listening to the sound of chewing inside my head. The salty cracker stung my tongue, soothed by the comforting, slippery sardine oil. Without thinking, I wiped a small drip off my lip with the back of my hand, then realized I couldn't rub it off on my pants. I left it, careful not to touch anything.

A neighbor's car drove by, crunching over the alley gravel. We waved sheepishly. We were the Back Door Boys. Porch Rebels.

I kept an eye on Dad's hands, watching every gesture in case I might need it one day. I smelled his after-shave. I selected another sardine, careful not to spill a drop lest I forever stink up this perfect moment.

COTTON CANDY: INTO THIN AIR

Me at the Buffalo County Fair, 1972: "Can I please have some cotton candy?"

Dad: "No."

"Pleeeeeze? Pleeeaaaauuuuzzhh?" As if adding syllables would help.

"No."

" I won't ask for any…"

"Fine — just shut up. Here's fifty cents. Go."

"It costs seventy-five cents, Dad."

"What? Seventy-five cents?! For *air*? For *sugar air*?"

I hold my ground silently. Dad flips me another quarter.

The best part of getting cotton candy is watching them make it. It can't be concocted in advance — it's too fragile and spoils too fast. They have to summon it like a swami before your very eyes.

First, they heat sugar in the middle of a device that looks like an empty washing machine tub. A needle valve spins, flinging thin strands of sugar-glue into the open drum, whipping the sweet stuff senseless until its natural crystalline structure is beat apart.

Troll-doll pink hairs start appearing, ghost-like along the edges, growing like a fast-motion spiderweb.

With a few deft twists of the wrist, the vendor whisks a long cardboard paper tube through the air, gathering and cultivating strands on his baton like an orchestral conductor, building to a towering crescendo: he hands me a teetering pile of Barbie-colored sparkle as upswept and awesome as grandma's beehive hairdo.

The cotton candy machine debuted to public awe at the 1904 World's Fair in St. Louis. Its inventor, William Morrison, was a dentist.[12] He gave his creation the unappetizing name "Fairy Floss."

Cotton candy is 100% sugar. Sugar is hydroscopic: get cotton candy wet and it shrinks immediately back into crystals like the devil recoiling from holy water. I spit onto my cotton candy to watch it retreat in craters, fairy-floss pink collapsing into blood-red drops stuck like flies in a web.

I couldn't bite into my cotton candy because the cloud of it was bigger than my head, so I'd tear furry strips away like corpse skin and stuff them in my mouth.

Nothing there.

I saw it go in. Yet my mouth was empty.

Another big wad crams in. The cotton candy disappears before I can chew it even once, dissolving into wee drops of gritty sugar spit. My teeth turn red. They sting. August flies abandon the blobs of ice cream spilled on the fairway dirt in favor of my sticky face. The giant cloud of pink sugar-air is soon gone, leaving nothing but a sticky cardboard tube, fuzzy-bald as an old man's head.

There are a thousand disappointments for a small boy. This is one.

Perhaps it hadn't been quite nothing. I began to feel a ringing in my ears and an acute mental clarity, followed by hyper-alertness. I became extremely focused and energized. In a rush of renewed hyperactivity, I headed straight for the Zipper.

---

12 It figures.

The Zipper was my favorite amusement park ride. It's a combination of Ferris Wheel, bulldozer track, shark cage and blender. It is an assault on all your senses as you somersault from 200 feet in the air toward the littered ground, an end-over-end tumble that rips coins from your pockets and then pelts you with them as if you were inside a popcorn popper.

Although I've eaten seemingly nothing, I get queasy, then barf. Pinwheels of pink gastrointestinal lacquer fling through the cage grate out across the midway. The clanging of loose coins quiets as they begin sticking to the gluey gum that lines the ceiling and floor of my chamber. I watch passively, heavy-lidded, noting idly that some of the coins and candy wrappers are not mine. I become dimly aware of the collage of matchbook covers and ticket stubs stuck to the periphery of my cage, a scrapbook of previous thrill-seekers.

The ride stops with a yank. The carny unlocks my cage door, my seatbar raises itself. My bare white legs make a Velcro sound as I peel myself off the red vinyl seat. A dollar's worth of pennies, nickels and dimes are stuck on me like campaign buttons. Halfheartedly I stoop to pry a few of my coins off the floor, but the attendant barks at me to move along. I clear out, making room for the next in line: a pink, pimple-faced boy, stoic as a soldier awaiting D-Day. He tears at a giant cloud of cotton candy.

"Next."

BIRTH ORDER

I am my mother's fifth child. There are six. The firstborn, my eldest brother, is only seven years older than me. That's how cute my mom is.

My little sister is ten years younger. I think it took ten years before it became apparent to my folks that they hadn't gotten a kid quite right yet.

The oldest — we'll call him "Ken," because that's his name — was always the smartest. Scholarships, class president, front man of a rock band. He was hard to hate. As I grew long and lanky like he was, with the same stooped shoulders and head-bobbing walk, I secretly liked it when people called me Ken. I liked it less when, as I grew my hair out long like his, a few people called me Patty. My sister Patty didn't like it much either. As an adult she admitted to me that she had spent a considerable amount of her childhood rifling through my parents' dresser drawers looking for proof that she was adopted.

My dad traveled a lot, which I guess is why he regularly referred to me as KenChuckCherylPatMick, with an instant blink of correction between each name. At least he got everybody in the right order. When my little sister was born, he got her name right on the first try, probably because he'd had a decade to sort us out. He wanted to name her Jodi, but my mother refused. They agreed on JoEllen Marie. Everyone calls her Jodi. If Ken were to step out in front of a bus, my family would unanimously name Jodi as the smartest, and not just because Ken was gone, but because you lose smart points for stepping out in front of a bus.

Not long after Jodi was born, I was cheerfully reciting the names of all the kids in my family in my little 10-year-old voice. "Ken, Chuck, Cheryl, Patty… Jodi…"

The sing-song stopped. I knew there were six kids. I went back through the names, feeling a little sheepish at first. Ken. Chuck, Cheryl. Patty. Jodi… Who was I missing? After a moment, unstoppable hot tears pressed out of my eyes. I hated myself. How could I be so thoughtless and self-centered that I didn't even remember all my brothers and sisters? In shame I confessed it to my mother, so desperate was I to find out whom I had forgotten that I was willing to reveal to her that her youngest son was a selfish moron.

She waited a few moments for me to figure it out. I didn't. She blinked at me, sweetly at first, then blankly. Out of pity she eventually added, "You forgot Mickey."

I think it is to my credit that the relief I felt to learn I hadn't forgotten anyone outweighed the embarrassment of being dim.

Perhaps someday I'll be the smartest kid in my family. It'll take a whole fleet of buses.

IN THE REAL WORLD

I waited in the wet alley behind the movie theater. It was a small-town venue, and its alley, lined with saggy cobblestones, was barely wide enough for the garbage truck to get through. I stood alone, waiting for the actors to come out.

At eight years old, I wasn't old enough to figure out how they projected actors onto the big screen. I figured they lit them from behind with a big lamp, and the shadows shined hard enough on the silky screen that the audience could see their enlarged images, much as my shadow from the streetlight was longer than I was.

Before the movie had started, a pleasant man in a bow tie had walked out from behind the curtain onto the stage. He mentioned a few upcoming attractions, encouraged us all to buy popcorn during the intermission, and then, after expressing his sincere hope that we would enjoy the film, he slipped behind the curtain into the dark, secret backstage world. I watched for him but he never appeared in the movie. He must have just sat back there the whole time, out of the way, his job complete.

I was lost in thought when the back door finally opened, and it made me jump. A man walked out with two garbage bags dripping with wet popcorn and sticky paper cups. I tried to steal a glimpse through the door before it closed, hoping for a peek at the movie set, the characters lounging around with their feet up, smoking. Maybe they'd see me and invite me in. But it was dark inside. I couldn't see anything before the door shut.

I walked slowly the three long blocks home. I do my best thinking when I walk. I sat down cross-legged beside our black-and-white TV, it's skinny legs nearly touching mine. I leaned over and considered its cross-section. There was clearly not enough room for anyone to be inside. I didn't know how they pulled it off, but that's when I realized I'd be had. The TV that took a place of honor in our crowded living room was a big liar, and I had waited in the alley for no one.

I had had my suspicions, but TV was otherwise filled with such trustworthiness: Andy Griffith, Captain Kangaroo, *Family Affair's* Uncle Bill and the nice father of Chip, Robbie and Ernie on *My Three Sons,* who also seemed to be the dad to half the families on *The Wonderful World of Disney* every Sunday night. That should have been another clue.

"Move back from the TV — you'll ruin your eyes," my mom warned. Still, every day I sat within touching distance of the bulging green glass, pixels big as my finger, and she didn't bother to repeat herself.

Each afternoon included a half-hour Bingo show. Mom would set me up with a few Bingo cards and a jar of dried beans. I listened dutifully to the voice on the TV as he read, "I...17. G...46." For those of you who are younger, this was high TV drama in the 1960s. I don't think I liked playing Bingo as much as I was compelled to organize beans perfectly centered into each square. If I completed a row, I knew to say *bingo!* but at that time of day I was alone in the living room, and the TV show continued as if I hadn't said anything.

I had a crush on the pretty teacher on *Romper Room*. Miss Linda presided over a tiny class of children I hadn't seen in town. She looked like Carol Burnett with black hair, her big toothy smile filled with kindness. At the end of each show she raised her Magic Mirror and looked deeply into it. After a few disorienting moments of wavy special effects, she could see right through the mirror, right through the TV and out into the world. "I see Bobby," she said. "I see Jane, and there's Debbie, and Tim."

I waited, staring, unblinking.

"…Rachel, and Kent, Eric and Susie…"

I waved meekly.

"…Abdul, LaTravia, Pedro, Ingrid…"

She went through every conceivable name, looking right at me, *right at me,* with that insipid smile even as she ignored me.

"It's Mickey!" I called out. "I'm *right here!*"

The credits rolled. I turned off the set, watching the image implode into a tiny star that dimmed like my joy until it vanished altogether. I sat more alone than before.

Not long after, I announced I would start going by my given name, Michael. My mom tried to be respectful of my wishes. To this day my siblings still call me Mickey. Until he died, my dad stumbled through all the names, "KenChuckCherylPatMick… uh, Mike."

I've learned that every fifth person shares my name. When I hear someone call "Mike!" my chemistry jumps a little but I don't turn around. They're usually calling for some other Mike, and I hate to be embarrassed by my anticipation, like waving back at someone who isn't waving at you.

Maybe when Miss Linda said "…and I see Billy," Billy wasn't sure she meant *him* Billy. But at least he could imagine it. He could continue to feel assured that Miss Linda was real, and with her acknowledgment, that he was too.

POLL POSITION

When I was a kid I marched up and down the sidewalk in front of my house carrying a "Richard Nixon for President" sign. I didn't really know who Nixon was—I was only nine years old—but I knew there was an election, and during elections people marched around. I found the sign in someone's garbage in our alley, and I liked marching around.

His opponent must have been be born for public service, because his name was McGovern. On the other hand, Nixon's running mate was Spiro Agnew, a name that's an anagram of "Gains Power." Plus, one of my favorite toys was a Spirograph. So having those perfectly good reasons for choosing a Commander in Chief with our nation and my future in his hands, I was a Nixon man.

A lot of public officials get elected thanks to such associations. For a while, just being named Kennedy got you a good government job. Back then no one even asked if you were related to *the* Kennedys, or whether you could keep your hands to yourself and your car out of the river.

But the times, they were a-changin'. Caroline Kennedy, as poised and elegant and toothful as her father John F. Kennedy, was blindsided in 2009 when reporters asked her why she thought she deserved to inherit Hillary Clinton's newly-vacated Senate seat. A moment passed, her eyes went blank. She mumbled, "Kennedy?" It wasn't enough any more. Polling numbers plummeted and she withdrew from the race for "personal reasons," which is what politicians say instead of "I quit."

Nobody was prepared for that. Unrelated Kennedys across the country blanched at the implication: they might actually have to be For Something. It began to spread, first to the Rockefellers, Roosevelts and Cheneys, then down to the Udalls, Cavanaughs and Kellys.

Barack Obama became President of the United States and proved that votes matter. His followers created change by getting out of their La-Z-Boys and making a difference. More people voted for him, and so he won, despite his middle name, Hussein. Holy cow, the system works! You can get what you want. Who knew?

Then after seven-and-a-half years in office, Supreme Court Justice Antonin Scalia died, and the leader of the Senate Judiciary Committee, a tricky aw-shucks Iowan named Chuck Grassley, refused to schedule a confirmation of Obama's new court nominee, Merrick Garland. Grassley said it was an election year and we should wait to hear the voice of the people. So never mind the Constitution, which he once swore to uphold: who did Chuck think elected President Obama in the first place? So the system didn't work. It began to look very, very broken.

I still love the Spirograph. I'll even march around holding a sign once in a while when the cause moves me. But I hope voters in future elections think deeper than I once did about why they're waving a sign, and whether the name on it really stands for what the sign does.

KIDDIE PORN

It took me a moment to realize that what I was seeing was not the overhead shot of a cooking show. Without introduction (which is to say, without *warning*), the video began with an opened kneecap surrounded by pulsing red meat and cream-white gristle. A magnified pair of tweezers and two gleaming silver picks were rearranging this tendon and that, as one might pick through a plate of spaghetti.

Terry Johnson has been my best friend since junior high school. Like any good friend, he mailed me a VCR tape of his knee surgery. TJ is proud of his knee, but *man*, I didn't need to see that.

I felt the same way in the fifth grade when a kid named Greg pulled a folded photo out of his pocket as if it were a hundred dollar bill. It had been pressed flat by his humid wallet. The magazine ink was beginning to smudge from being sat on. He opened it delicately, its folded edges worn white.

It took me a few seconds to orient, to make sense of the bright spotlight glare on the greasy body hair and sweat.

Greg grinned, as if he carried the golden ticket to eternal friendship. Greg was a creep.

I responded with an uncommittal "Huh…" before handing it back, subconsciously wiping my hands on my pants. This was exactly the kind of thing I always got caught doing when it wasn't my idea.

OF MICE AND ME

Porn and I got off to a bad start.[13] I stumbled across images here and there, and I'd tear out the ones that intrigued me and save them. Eventually, I had a little private collection of clippings. I shared a room with my brother, so I could never admire my art with him around. He'd rat me out just for the fun of watching me run for my life. When I wanted to view my collection, I'd gather them carefully and slink into the bathroom, the only room in our house with a door that locked. With two parents and six kids sharing the house, visits to the only bathroom had to be judicious.

I've since wondered how the person reacted, who was next into the bathroom the day I accidentally left my collage behind. I didn't discover my blunder until hours later. I rushed back in to the bathroom, but they were gone.

The obvious choice for my parents would have been to punish my older brother, because they never accepted that I was old enough to do the things I did. I was eighteen before my dad realized I had a driver's license and could play guitar. My brother, though, showed no signs of having been beaten. Nor did he beat me in revenge, or reveal any hint that he found the photos himself: no smirk, no teasing, no long trips of his own to the bathroom. If my sisters had discovered them, there would have been screams, flames, bazookas. Perhaps God intervened and whisked them away in the wind, a blessing for all of us.

As I got older, I confiscated whole magazines. There was an abandoned school stadium near my house where my friend Harold and I stashed our contraband. It was more fun to have a forbidden hoard than to actually look at the magazines. Old magazines acquire a unique smell when they are stored in dank places. The pages turn to clay. To this day I think antique stores smell like porn.

---

13 I got the hang of it eventually.

I don't remember how I got the magazines, and I don't remember what became of them. In the world of pubescent boys, things just come and go. When I was thirteen I had access to a tandem bicycle, and when I was fourteen I didn't. I don't know why or whose it was. Probably the booty was discovered and stolen by younger explorers starving for education.

Given their exaggerated proportions everywhere else, Barbie and Ken were surprisingly plain under their disco duds. Smooth, featureless skin with nothing at their nethers but the joint of their legs. I know that some families parade around naked all the time, but my family was a buttoned-up bunch, so I had to learn anatomy the hard way.

My first hands-on experience provided little revelation. I found myself cruising up and down Central Avenue in tan Cutlass driven by a girl from the neighboring town. We parked in a grocery store lot and kissed. She wanted my class ring. Was my hand under her bra, or wasn't it? It was hard to tell. She felt as smooth and plastic as Barbie. It took me a while to realize she had Band-Aids over her nipples. A hundred reasons raced around my imagination before she offered that her mother made her wear them.

I replied, "Oh, yeah," as if her explanation cleared anything up. Sometimes by acting as if I understood something, I'd gather enough clues along the way to make sense of it. I'm still gathering.

Two years later, to everyone's surprise, our small town theater booked an X-rated film. Curtis, who once confided in me that he aspired to be a mortician so he could see women naked, swore he could get us in with fake IDs. We rehearsed the suavity required to saunter into the lobby like we belonged there. When my friend passed out our IDs, mine was for a 45-year-old Hispanic who was a foot shorter and forty pounds heavier than I was.

I looked up from my new ID to meet the eyes of the ticket-taker. He was my next door neighbor. He eyed me, looked at my ID and said, "You gotta be kidding." I was dead. "Enjoy the show, Mr. Rodriquez," he hissed through grinning teeth, rolling his eyes and waving me in.

The movie was about as sexy as The Three Stooges, but not as funny. I vaguely recall a scene with two hairy trapeze artists, one hanging upside down, connecting and unconnecting with a *pop* sound as they swung. The more I saw, the less I wanted to learn. It ended forever my dreams of running off and joining the circus.

The first drive-in movie of each season was usually a racy one, and if one rode one's bike down a certain street, one could glimpse the screen over the fence. I made the guilty trip and parked as long as I dared. Without access to the soundtrack sent through the metal car-window speaker, I surmised that the plot centered around an enormously endowed woman seeking revenge as a serial suffocator.

I don't know what became of leering little Greg and his folded up photos. Maybe he opened a newsstand of his own. Curtis abandoned his mortician dream and became a wealthy business analyst instead. In spite of all my informal education, I think I turned out okay too.

BRAIN PAIN

I can't remember a time in my life when I didn't ache in one spot or another. I just healed up my right shoulder, and now my left one has sprung a spring.

I didn't *do* anything to it. It just started hurting. A lot. Maybe I brushed my teeth too hard, or slept funny. But there was no *poink* moment.

I've always had bruises and dings. Tall, bony and clumsy, I constantly hit my head, stumbled down stairs, fell off my bicycle, or slid down a ditch while on wayward rollerskates.[14] Those bonks and twists are earned honestly, a badge I wear that reminds me I was *doing* something. I'm far less tolerant of aches that just show up on their own, like uninvited guests who won't go home.

My shins never had any meat on them. It is a deformity. They're as bumpy and raw as a tree branch. You can read every woody detail of my shin bone like the rings of a tree, or like that clear plastic Invisible Man we played with in elementary school, the one with realistic organs on the inside and the missing organ on the outside. During a softball game I once took an errant pitch to the shin, and from the sound it made, everyone thought I got a hit.

In the middle of the city park near my childhood home, there was a circular stone building that housed some mysterious municipal

---

14 These are not random examples.

function. We had no idea what caused the droning hum that came from inside, like the background noise in the lab from the original movie *Frankenstein*. Although we could climb the walls, we couldn't see through the dirty windows. The outside had a rocky facade rough enough to get a toe-hold, a natural scaling wall up to the tempting flat roof with its castle-like edge teeth, beguiling as Rapunzel.

My friend Eric scampered up the rocks like a gecko. "I did it! You do it!" he crowed, a phrase that has led countless children to their deaths. Scared of heights but more afraid of taunting, I slowly worked my way up, eventually squirming over the square roof edge like a fat raccoon.

I made it! The view was heady. Squirrels were eye-level. The passing clouds felt closer.

Going down was a lot scarier than climbing up. Eric, his face scrunched in concentration, worked his way down. Eric was small and lithe, the kind of kid who could get away with teasing you because you could never get a good enough grip on him to pound him. I was as graceful as a can of Pick-Up Sticks. Barely able to breathe, I managed to work my way over the edge, fingernails digging into the rock, to a ledge halfway down. Unable to feel a way beyond it and mindful of the setting sun, I jumped the remaining twelve feet or so. I felt a ringing in my feet as all the cartilage melted into Jello. I froze in place, afraid to walk or lay down.

"If you're not going to do it, get off!" Another magic phrase to kill children, and Eric barked it impatiently. I had determined, hypothetically, that by releasing one's hand from the chain one could do a back flip off the park swing at the apex of its arc. I was psyching myself up to prove it. *Just lean backwards and let go of the chains,* I said to my body, but my hands would not obey. I wanted to rehearse it in my mind a few more times, but Eric began his nagging. I kicked my head back into the reverse-somersault maneuver as the swing reached its breathtaking height. My hands still did not let go, not until I had completed my rotation and the swing began returning to Earth. Now I had the saddle in front of me. I continued to rotate as I finally releasing the chains, landing on my back with a dull *huff!* Everything sounded muffled after that. I don't remember walking home.

The next day I returned to the spot, with Eric on my left side and a new white cast on my right. Pressed into the hardened dirt was an imprint of my forearm, and we admired how the wrist turned at an impossible angle. Eric's head resonated like a ripe melon when I tapped it with my cast.

My nose looks like my dad's, long and with seductive curves that favor the left side of my face. His had been broken by the first punch of his first boxing match of his first week of the Navy. But one does not inherit a broken nose.

"Dad," I asked, "did I ever break my nose too?" I tried not to stare at his.

"No, no," he replied after a thoughtful, eye-wandering silence. "I don't recall anything,"

"Then how come my nose is so crooked?"

"Well," he said, scratching his beard, "there was that one time when you were three, and you walked in front of a kid wearing steel-toed boots who was swinging on the swing. He kicked you in the face, and you did a back flip, landing right back on your feet. Darndest thing."

Yeah, Dad — that might be it.

Or maybe it was Plunger. Plunger was one of the the pile-on games we played in the park after school. Kids on one team would form a human chain by lining up, bending over and wrapping arms firmly around the waist of the next kid in front, who did the same. It looked like a caterpillar or a woven rope. The forward-most kid would steady himself by wrapping his arms around a tree. The other team would run up one at a time and dive onto the fortified mass of humanity, using their cumulative weight and relentless impacts to collapse the wall. Your score per round was how many kids your team held up. To protect the tree-grabbing kid's collar bone, we'd insert the littlest kid as padding between him and the tree trunk. He was the Plunger.

I only recall playing the game twice. The second time, while I was in the middle of the wall team, we held up a record number of opponents before the entire matrix of kids collapsed on top of my nose.

Nose blood is especially red from all the fresh oxygen. Instinctively the other kids all ran home.

As I get older, I play less. Yet my injuries continue. I scratched my cornea on a juniper branch when I picked up a basketball. While backing up my car, I turned my head to look behind me and sprained my neck. I pulled a muscle in my shoulder lifting a saucer out of the dishwasher.

It's as if my body is accustomed to feeling injured, and continues out of habit. It says to itself,

> *Say, it's about time for a sprung knee, isn't it?*
> *No, knees are Monday.*
> *Foot cramp?*
> *Foot cramps are Friday. It's Tendon Tuesday.*
> *Okay. Here goes…*

Oww! What did I do?

THAT'S SNOW BIZ

A blizzard was coming. With great anticipation I waxed up my old sled, the red paint on its metal runners long since worn off by dry patches of ground. My mother was looking at my thin corduroy jacket, its sleeves ending closer to my elbows than my wrists. Another growth spurt. "We need to get you a new winter coat," she sighed. I had been oblivious, but could see she was right. She sent me out into the blizzard with Dad.

This was a big event. We weren't poor, but there were six of us kids and we didn't get a lot of new stuff. Snorkel-hood parkas were the fad, and Dad let me try one on. It had sleeves that covered my whole arm, and a fur-trimmed hood that rolled out so far and long that my face was tucked in deep as a bear cave.

Still in the store, I buttoned every button and zipped its many zippers, then like an astronaut on his first spacewalk I ventured out into the storm. The ring of the dangling bell over the door was drowned out by the fierce wind. White razors of snow cut across my tunnel vision, but I didn't feel a thing. This was what Eskimos see, the view through the door of their igloos. I stepped back inside, wide-eyed with feelings of invincibility. I was afraid to say "Thank you," fearful that speaking might spoil my lucky streak.

I grew up in a smallish Nebraska town. (They all are.) Planted randomly on the flat prairie like a salt shaker on a tabletop, the town took the full brunt of storms as they built speed, unobstructed by the treeless landscape. The next morning the wind stopped and the white sun drilled a hole through the blue sky, blindingly reflecting off the crystal snow two feet thick. The town bogged to a halt, the muffled quiet interrupted only by the occasional whine of spinning tires.

My friend Harold had a snorkel-hood parka too. We grabbed shovels and headed out to save the world. We got ten dollars for each sidewalk we shoveled. Digging out a stuck car usually scored a five dollar tip. It was more money than I had ever seen. Any money you make as a kid is a fortune, because someone else is cooking for you, paying your rent, taking care of your utilities, clothing, and medical expenses. If you make ten bucks, your net gain is *ten bucks*.

Shoveling snow was a goldmine. The reason I don't do it today is because I have learned kids will still do it for ten bucks.

Playing in the snow evolved over time. I went from making snow angels to stockpiling snowballs, which took some adjustment because I wore mittens my mom had knitted for me. Snow sticks to yarn like Velcro. It is a sad, demeaning walk when you hit someone with a snowball and then you have to trudge over to them and ask for your mitten back.

I graduated from a saucer sled to a classic wooden runner, a hand-me-down from my brothers and, for all I know, from my dad before that. It sported a T-bar that steered by warping the skinny metal runners into an arc. My friends made fun of it, richer kids who always had the latest plastic junk. But they always wanted to borrow mine after I blew past them on the hill. The wood and steel didn't break like the brittle cold plastic sleds, and so I never got a new one. Eventually I grew too long for the sled, but we were frugal and never threw anything away that was still good.

My final high school sled was my dad's Datsun B-210. I'd throw the tiny car into wild, dizzying spins on the parking lot ice, something I stopped doing after I bought my own car.

I took up cross-country skiing, a great sport for people who don't mind being face-down in the snow. Once in Colorado I broke through the snow's crust and found myself waist deep, unable to move my feet. The forest was so quiet I felt as if my head was expanding. I took out a pad and pencil and wrote an entire song while standing stuck in the snow. It's a pretty good song, but no matter how I analyze it, it has nothing to do with snow. Still, I thought it would be a hit, because nothing generates buzz like a musician found frozen to death with a song clutched in his fist.

Today I prefer snow cannons. While preparing for an upcoming blizzard, I broke my little 17-year-old snowblower trying to get it started, and had to rush out into the face of the impending storm to get a new one. Everyone else must have broken theirs an hour before I did, because the only snowblowers left at the store were overpowered and expensive—all the cute little ones were gone. It's hard to dicker with a snowblower salesman who only has two left, the TV above your head is squealing about the impending blizzard and a line of impatient buyers is fidgeting behind you.

I swallowed hard and bought a big one. It has an electric starter, but you have to plug it in to use it. It takes longer to plug it in than to just pull the starter rope, but I use the electric starter anyway because I paid for it. The behemoth belches, barks, then settles to a manly purr at my finger's touch, and nearly drives itself through the garage door.

It has a cannon barrel you aim by turning a crank, like the turret of a tank. It has two speeds just for reverse, so you can run over yourself fast or slow.

OF MICE AND ME

I couldn't wait to get my testosterone all over it. Unfortunately, the blower was so big the job was finished quicker than I was ready for. Reluctantly, I followed it back to the garage, loitering a bit hoping to blow more snow on stuff. I was cold too, and that surprised me. Usually I work up a good sweat. But I had only followed this machine around, pointing it toward the real work as if I were a union boss. I was dry and comfortable, and the snow I used to play in was piled neatly out of reach. What's the fun in that?

But finally it came: the big wet dump. A foot of back-breaking, heavy snow. Those cute little blowers gagged and choked. Out came shovels, then Tylenol. But my fire-engine red Mr. Big leaned in, humming just a little deeper as it tossed a solid bar of snow over its shoulder, chewing a perfect trough through the mess.

Three days later, another foot of snow. And another a few weeks later. Plows were burying crosswalks without a thought to the heroic efforts of homeowners trying to keep them open. Neighbors gave up, resigned to wait for spring.

In my head I composed a superhero theme song and hummed it to myself as I donned my snowsuit, gearing up like an astronaut for a stroll on the Moon. I felt like a god with a magic wand, parting the white ocean so my people could pass, through the crosswalks, across the street, up the neighbor's driveway, then two more driveways. Maybe I spent 500 calories steering the behemoth, but I gained 1000 in a big bundt cake a neighbor brought over in gratitude. I don't know how other superheroes stay skinny enough for all that Spandex.

Does Batman get bored and lonely when trouble quiets? Does he wish for a dust-up, for a robber to yank a little old lady's purse? Because I know I'm hoping for a big fat dump of snow, just like when I was a kid.

THE FUNERAL PROCESSION

PART I

I was barely sixteen when I attended my first funeral. It was in honor of my friend Jimmy whom I had met just three weeks earlier. My parents encouraged me to go, but didn't offer to accompany me. I drove the seven quiet miles to Gibbon, Nebraska alone.

I didn't know what to expect. I was apprehensive, in a fog. I hadn't yet learned how to cry in public.

I don't remember who first introduced me to Jimmy, but we hit it off immediately. He was a drummer, and his country band needed a new guitar player. I fancied myself to be a rock guitarist, but Jimmy swore the band was really fun, and they were booked solid for a year. The rock band I was trying to start had played one gig in a year, with nothing more in sight.

I auditioned for his band, played them a song or two, and they hired me on the spot. "Come here on Saturday and I'll drive you to the gig," said the leader, Don. Don was half black, half Mexican, with a strong limp to remind him of the polio he had forty years earlier. His black eyes always sparkled, and his smile cocked to one side. He was a natural frontman. Like Joe Cocker, it was hard to take your eyes off him.

"When do we rehearse?" I asked.

"It's *country*, son," Don said kindly. "We don't rehearse. Just play the songs. You'll be fine."

Jimmy gave me a grin that said, *See? How cool is that!*

By that weekend, Jimmy was in a coma. While driving his 5-year-old sister to school, his sweet Pontiac GTO was broadsided by a bread truck on a gravel road intersection so remote they didn't bother to use stop signs.

His mother sensed it. She rose from her desk at the packing plant, walked silently out of work and drove directly to the spot of the crash. She was the first to arrive.

Ten days later Jimmy was declared dead, and I was cobbling together appropriate clothes for his funeral. The first thing I saw when I entered the hall was Jimmy in his open casket. I froze in place. I had no idea people did such things. It was awful to stare, but I couldn't look away.

I inched closer, and it wasn't Jimmy after all, not really. I'm sure the mortician did his best, but Jimmy had been crushed, and the reconstruction was imperfect. Jimmy's head was now longer, narrower, more square. His brand new class ring dangled like a charm from his bony finger.

I don't remember much else. Words were said, they closed the lid, and hauled Jimmy away.

I stayed with this band of strangers for a couple of years, learning classics like *Lonesome 7-7203*, *The Key's in the Mailbox*, and *Crystal Chandelier*. I never told my rock-and-roll friends I was booked every weekend. My friends never saw the band photo, the four of us wearing matching brushed denim leisure suits, each of us leaning one hand on a photography studio fence, me half the age of the others.

Don eventually married Jimmy's mom and adopted his little sister, who had recovered from the accident as only a child can. Last time

I saw her, she squealed as she wedged herself four feet up inside a doorway, proud as a chimp, her grin tugged crooked by faint pink lines where her face had once been torn open. I like to think she's a raving beauty now, but I have no idea where any of them might be.

I moved away to college, eventually losing touch with them all.

So that was that.

PART II

I was lucky enough to go four years before my next funeral. I had a front row seat, a designated pall-bearer for a man I had never met.

How do you live 98 years and get carried out by a stranger? I didn't dwell on it. I answered yes when my father-in-law asked me to help. He was not close to the father he was burying, and probably didn't have an answer to that himself.

The funeral was held at St. Cecilia's Cathedral, among the largest, most breathtaking churches in the country. Although I had dabbled in quite a few denominations,[15] I was unfamiliar with Catholic rituals. Catholics save a special set of them for funerals. I nearly bolted from my pew when I glanced over my shoulder and caught three robed boys with spears advancing down the aisle. As the priest flicked holy water on the gleaming honey-maple casket, I had to nail my feet to the floor to stop from wiping it off. My brain screamed, *It'll ruin the finish!*

The priest gave a nod to the pall-bearers. I was port side and in front, so I couldn't watch the others for clues what to do. We lifted

---

15 I was raised a Methodist, where they baptize babies on the head – kind of a "good luck out there, kid" sort of thing. At 14 years old I became an atheist, sincerely believing that the entire creation story was man's description of aliens visiting Earth. In college I hung out at a Baptist church, but they wouldn't accept me until I got baptized a second time, because the first one didn't count. I eventually settled in a Christian Church, which is a fine denomination in spite of having the most generic name possible. Currently, I spend Sunday mornings making omelets and reading the paper.

the old man slowly while an attendant slipped the gurney away from underneath. I was surprised how light the casket felt, as if no one was inside.

St. Cecilia's Cathedral sits atop a grand procession of steep marble steps. As we passed outside through its giant iron doors and descended, I lifted the front of the casket slightly to keep it level. My starboard partner lifted in kind, but the two men in back instinctively lifted too instead of lowering, and the casket lurched head-first downhill, like a Soapbox Derby racer.

Before we had a chance to respond, I felt the wiry deceased slide with a *shish* across the slippery silk lining, down toward the bow of his ship. The shifting weight caused the rear of the casket to lurch upward even higher as his head konked against the front with a hollow melon thump. I nearly stumbled under the sudden weight shift, but with a quick heave we righted the ship.

As we reached the bottom step and aligned him for docking into the yawning hearse, my eyes darted around. Furtive looks danced among the pall-bearers, but not a word was said. We had been the first out the door — did no one else see it? The hearse's hatch closed with a quiet, final *chunk,* and off the old man went, his freshly pressed suit rumpled up around his chest, his elbows up around his ears, his head shoved sideways for eternity.

At the cemetery I stood beside my brother-in-law (another of the pall-bearers) whose crumpled grandfather was now suspended by steel cables over a fresh hole in the dark, wet earth. It was now or never.

"You felt…" I whispered.

"Yeah."

"You gonna say anything?"

"I dunno."

We waited, hands crossed in front of us, dark sunglasses hiding our eyes as we scanned the scene like FBI agents. The other pall-bearers must have known too, but we didn't make eye contact. What would be done, anyway? Stop the ceremony, pry open the casket, grab gramps by the ankles and yank him straight, tugging his suit back down over his waist, his pant legs down from his knees?

The grandson fidgeted and shrugged. Time decided for us as now-or-never became never. The casket began its descent, more water was sprinkled, prayers were mumbled, roses were tossed, dirt was flung.

And that was that.

MODEL BEHAVIOR

Alone in my bedroom, I was failing at gluing a tiny plastic shock absorber to its tiny axle. I had squirted far too much glue, a glob bigger than the two pieces combined. It was all over my fingers, making it impossible to stick anything together because it was all stuck to me. Floundering, I bumped my orange modeling paint off the desk and watched helplessly, my fingers glued together, as it poured out onto the thick beige carpet.

It was the kind of day-glo orange a nine-year-old kid would be drawn to. I dabbed some of it up with a rag until I got high from the fumes and gave up. I was dead. I left the rest to dry. I didn't ask for help, hoping that by ignoring it, it would just go away.[16] When I returned forty years later to help my mother move out of her house, I was surprised to see the stain was still there.

My favorite models were the Revells. A latticework frame held the wee pieces, to be twisted off and used to assemble my AMC Gremlin Funny Car or P-51 Mustang Fighter Plane. My most ambitious project was a complete Saturn V rocket with an Apollo module on top, that opened to reveal the Lunar Landing Module tucked authentically inside. I built this while NASA was building the real one. I learned a lot about rockets and modeling glue.

---

16 Kids don't really believe trouble will just go away, but without a better plan, they'll give it a shot.

I was glued to our black-and-white TV, hungry for every tidbit about the Apollo missions. I flew my LEM in front of the television as Apollo 11 landed on the Moon. Even as a kid I was amazed that someone had the foresight to install a camera on the landing module in order to film the historic "small step for a man," and in spite of all the required innovations in technology, the video was broadcast upside down.

I learned that Moon was also the maiden name of Buzz Aldrin's mother. I didn't learn she had committed suicide only a year before his historic flight, because they didn't tell kids that.

I wanted to be an astronaut. I was told I didn't have a chance because, at age 13 and only 130 pounds, I was already 6' 2", too tall to fit a jet or rocket.

I was also very interested in gymnastics — especially the parallel bars — but again they said I was too tall.

I also considered being a forest ranger, because I heard they gave you a truck, a radio and a cabin, and left you alone all winter. That sounded great, and you could be as tall as you pleased. But I was told that nobody from Nebraska would get into forestry school because it was competitive and they only accepted people from their own state. Nebraska had no forestry schools. The state has only one official forest, and it's man-made.

I majored in philosophy, until one of my professors jumped out a 13th-story window. I decided that whatever he had figured out, I didn't want to learn, so I switched to psychology, a department that had no height restrictions and was in a lower building.

While I was in college, 6' 2" Nebraska gymnast Bart Conner won a gold medal on the parallel bars in the Olympics. He had been in one of my classes.

OF MICE AND ME

That same year, 6' 2" astronaut Jim Weatherbee piloted the space shuttle Columbia, eventually becoming the first astronaut to command five flights.

When someone buys my mom's house, I bet the first thing they will do is tear up that spoiled carpet. No one will ever forget the Apollo astronauts, and if that spot had been Aldrin's footprint, they'd cut it out and frame it. As it is, the only thing lost is the legacy of one boy who dreamed of becoming an astronaut, but whose only mark in space exploration was an orange stain.

A MOVING DAY

My mother moved out of her house in my humble hometown of Kearney, Nebraska, after staying put for forty-eight years. I was two years old when we moved there, and I didn't leave until college beckoned. All six kids moved on. Dad passed away. Once a perpetual cacophony, the house had become every kind of empty.

You wouldn't think I'd remember anything about the house I lived in my first two years, but I do. I remember patches of grass in the back yard. I remember air vents in the middle of the second floor that you could peek through to spy on people in the living room below. I remember the long white station wagon parked outside, its green and white vinyl bench seat, the taste of its hard Bakelite plastic steering wheel with the bright chrome rocker arm that honked to my great delight when I leaned on it. I'm told I figured out how to shift the car into neutral, and took it for a roll down the hill with my five-year-old sister beside me, avoiding disaster on the busy cross street below only when my brother dove through the window and pulled the parking brake. But I don't remember any of that, and don't trust it because the hero of the story is the one who told it to me.

The Kearney home is where my life was.

After forty-eight years, a house collects a lot of personal stuff. Each of Mom's kids had his own stash, boxes left behind as we crept out into the world. After much fair warning, mother carted most of it off to various thrift stores. I wonder what became of my complete Matchbox car collection? Too late to do anything about it now. Some lucky 3-year-old is probably sticking my 1971 Silver Boss Hoss Mustang in his mouth. Or some 50-year-old is sticking it on eBay.

I returned to my hometown to help Mom sort things out. Dad had died a few years before, but much of his stuff was right where he left it.

When you're moving, everything becomes sentimental. It's hard to get started. Everything you pick up has a story that you stop to share. "Oh! I remember this stapler! I stapled myself to the davenport with it!"

I was assigned to clear out the basement, a great starter job since I'd be alone and could find my emotional footing. It was the Midwestern kind of basement, with a separate cellar door angled nearly flat to the ground. Like Dorothy in *The Wizard of Oz,* you bent down to open it, and just like the movie you usually had to kick it a time or two to break it loose from the spiderwebs and dust.

It opened with a horror movie *squeeeek* to reveal a dark cinderblock descent down a heavy plank stairway. As a boy I was certain that somehow I would fall — or be dragged — through the open spaces between every step. I often descended sitting down, sliding gingerly over each splintery plank to the underworld.

At the bottom was a strong wooden door with heavy crossbeams, like you see at the home of the Frankensteins. The dark, unfinished oak was rock hard. The original black doorknob, now 120 years old, was secured with a deadbolt on the inside. We were warned from birth to keep it locked. I imagined a hundred reasons why.

From the outside, it was wise to open the door slowly because on the reverse side hung a dartboard. The inside face of the door was pocked with a thousand misses, evidence that we were a family of lousy shots. Had we been hunters, we would have starved long ago.

The door shut with a deep ka-*chunk*. And there I was, in the silent, unfinished basement. As my eyes adjusted, a spray-painted skeleton leered from the wall, a remnant of the single Halloween party we hosted. The creepy basement, draped in cobwebs and dark beams, hardly needed decorating. Yet in rare abandon, my father sprayed graffiti ghouls across the west wall, across the cellar door, down the south wall. I was aghast, and thrilled.

There were still a few toys and games down there, the destructive kind like darts that weren't allowed in the rest of the house. My Hot Wheels track, which benefited from all that unobstructed floor space, had been kept down there too, but now most of the shelves were vacant and dusty.

I crept silently over the stairway landing to the Holiest of Holies: my father's workshop.

I walked reverently, just as I had as a kid in my little Keds, shy to disturb anything, as one might explore a funeral home. The room had a slight powdery sheen of honey-colored wood dust, and the floor was a scrapbook of paint drips.

I gave wide berth to the Radial Arm Saw of Death and passed Dad's Wall of Tools. Dad bought any tool he thought he *might* need, regardless of whether there was any immediate purpose. "You never know." Like the tiny mirror with a curved handle that let you peer into awkward spaces to find the ring you dropped down the heating grate. Or the two-feet-long, spindly picker-upper-grabber thing, a syringe-type plunger on one end and a little claw on the other, to reach deep and retrieve that ring. Or the polishing wheel made of lamb's wool to shine it back up.

Most of his tools offered services which were never called upon. Once you had a tool to retrieve a lost ring, you never lost a ring. But you never know.

OF MICE AND ME

A cardinal sin against my father was Failure to Return a Tool to Where it Belongs. He had traced each tool's shape on the pegboard wall with a marker. A missing tool stood out as accusingly as a homicide outline on the sidewalk.

I passed the double-wheel grinder, an irresistible tool perfect for sharping darts. It spat radiant blue and gold sparks with a screech I think of every time I'm in a subway. It's the kind of tool that makes a kid look for things to sharpen.

I reached the scrap room. Dad never threw away a piece of wood larger than a quarter. "You never know." He stacked everything neatly: large planks there, small slivers here, old window frames and boxes in orderly piles that made sense only to him. It was dark, even with the light on, draped in cobwebs and crickets. Rough and broken edges poked out like greedy fingers. As a kid my heart would race as I stood in the middle of it all, as if I could summon the pieces to swirl up into a living whole. I was certain that with the right parts and the right tools I could build myself a wooden bicycle. I would select a single dusty plank, pick out a screw from Dad's infinite library of spare hardware, and twist it into the wood. I'd back the screw out and put it away again.

Every night after dinner, Dad would slip down to the basement and tinker. I think he needed the time alone, but he wouldn't deny me if I crept down to watch his thick, wrinkly fingers deftly dance over some intricate project, a single bead of sweat always hanging from the tip of his nose as he patiently explained how to use whatever tool he was holding. Just by watching, I eventually learned how to sharpen a knife on a whetstone, how to sweat a copper pipe, cut a miter joint, solder an electrical wire, and curse.

He taught me to respect the Radial Arm Saw of Death by relating a story of his old shop teacher who had lost an index finger in a moment of inattention. After the man recovered, he decided to use the sorry accident as a teaching moment. He demonstrated to the class the wrong way to hold a small piece of wood across the saw, and lopped off another finger.

I found Dad's old Dremel set with its tiny saws and odd-shaped grinding bits, all organized in an army-green metal case. It looked like a toy, but he never let me play with it — another reason I can still count to ten on my fingers. I never once saw him use it.

The first time I heard my baby sister laugh out loud was through the floor vent from the living room above. Dad paused the polishing of a brass doorknob, elbowed me and pointed at the ceiling with his eyes, then winked at me as her belly laugh infected me with giggles.

The first time I felt like a grown-up was when Dad borrowed my hammer. I bought my own for a high-school Construction Technology class. Twenty sixteen-year-old morons built a house from scratch every year. We swung screaming circular saws with abandon and learned to adjust a nail gun so it wouldn't shoot clear through a beam and into someone on the other side. The only requirements for the class: a hammer and a pencil.

I was proud of my hammer. It was flashy red, with a "low-vibration" ergonomic fiberglass handle. My Dad's wood hammer looked frumpy in comparison.

While I coveted my hammer, I never remembered to bring a pencil to class. No one did. The teacher would tell us to help measure something, and be met with blank looks all around.

"Pencil? Anyone?"

Silence.

"Out of all you guys, there isn't one pencil?"

We'd borrow his. "Who has The Pencil?"

I left home for college, although I came back every weekend. Then every other weekend. Then just major holidays. Building a life of my own, I went back over summer break to collect some of my things. My eyebrows raised as I spied my hammer dangling on his pegboard, with a black outline lassoed posessively around it. I thought about the dozen or so of his tools I'd lost in the back yard over the years. But the gene that says "don't mess with a man's tools" was switched on, leaving me with a whole new appreciation of my father.

After Dad died, my brother, who lives closest, would stop by to borrow his tools, and saw little point in returning them. When I came back to help clear out the house, Dad's pegboard was little more than petroglyphs of hammers and crowbars and levels, a game of *Operation* with all the bones missing.

I poked through little bins of miscellany, chatting with Dad out loud as I went. I chided him over the stuff he filed, like the coffee can marked "foam pieces."

Lining the bottom of a box of model plane parts, I found the original 1960 plans for his sailboat. There was a small picture in the corner, how the boat would look finished, launched off the dock by a proud skipper smoking a pipe. Dad took up pipe-smoking around then, and built that boat in the back yard. Later I found a photo of Dad looking exactly like that skipper as he coaxed his new boat off the dock for the first time.

Sketched in pencil on the back of those plans were his doodles of an iceboat he ended up building out of 4x4 beams. I found a few radio-controlled airplane flight logs. Dad didn't waste words. "Mar 28. Crashed. Heading home."

It took a day to sort out the rare treasures from rusty remnants destined for the thrift store or the garbage. I stacked a roomful of garbage bags to be hauled away. I fired up Dad's noisy Shop-Vac one last time to clear out his cobwebs and sawdust. Then the room was empty and silent.

Upstairs, Mom and my sister Patty were wrapping fine china plates I was seeing for the first time, and sorting through photographs. In all of those photographs I am above ground, but in most of my memories I'm in the basement.

Mom was grateful to have the basement chore off her mind. I took Dad's sailboat plans home to be ironed flat and framed, along with the matching photo of him on the finished boat.

A set of tiny jeweler's files from his basement are now in mine. I see them every day and marvel how his thick fingers ever managed such intricate tools. His Dremel box is on my shelf, and I don't use it any more than he did.

My hands look more like his now, although maybe not as strong — something I noticed as I hauled the garbage bags full of his stuff out through the old cellar door.

I never did build a wooden bicycle.

After I got home, I went to the hardware store to get a new lawn sprinkler. Like Dad, I took a long detour through the tool isle. Amid the screwdrivers and saw blades and drill bits, I spied a shiny "Combination Depth Gauge with Inside/Outside Calipers." With this tool one can measure (to a millimeter, thanks to its clever Vernier gauge) the width of a shaft, or the hole the shaft hopes to go into. I've never used such a caliper. Didn't know how to. Never needed one.

I bought it anyway.

You never know.

SOMETHING I ATE

TRENDING MARKETS

Here in the heartland of agriculture, we've cultured something that grows great on four acres of parking lot: the farmers market.

A farmers market isn't much of a market and doesn't include many farmers. Mostly it's rows of big white tents anchored with sandbags in case farm weather shows up. With all the tie-dye scarves and homemade herbal ointments for sale, most farmers markets look more like the merch table at a Phish concert.

The "farmers" are mostly handsome, fresh-looking kids in their twenties, draped in natural linen shirts and Ray-Bans. All the vendors have clean fingernails and wear earbuds. None are wearing Key overalls. They're all sunny and friendly. I like them. I just don't believe they're farmers.

I don't believe they're farmers because they sell tomatoes in April. They sell corn on the cob in May. They sell goat cheese even though nobody around here has seen a goat outside of a petting zoo.

The real farmers I know don't have time for a farmers market. They're too busy operating million-dollar self-steering GPS-enabled combines that harvest a 45-foot swath of genetically perfect corn which will be delivered direct and fresh to an ethanol factory. They're busy maintaining the machines that deliver a ton of hormonally-enriched by-products from the other end of the ethanol plant to feed a thousand chickens that have never seen grass and would be blinded by the bright sunshine reflecting off the pearl-white skin of a farmers market vendor.

On a real farm, you browse livestock. A friend recently went to a real farm to buy a guest of honor for his pig roast. "Which one do you like?" the farmer asked as they stood among the merchandise.

"You pick," my friend said to his young son. The boy pointed randomly at one unlucky pig. The farmer pulled out a pistol and shot it right in front of them.

That's a real farm.

At the farmers market you browse small-batch cheeses, hand-crafted in a small town in Iowa, not too far from a real farm. Each is lovingly hand-wrapped by a person who recently quit her executive vice president position at First Data.

There are various opportunities to sample the local Nebraska wines, which I often do to remind myself that there's still something to like about California.

I love the smell of steaming funnel cakes, which look a lot like farm fresh steaming cow pies.

I love the street music. It's not farmer music — these banjos and accordions and straw hats and zydeco are more like a Louisiana version of *Hee Haw*. I'm a little less enthusiastic about the prodigious three-year-old drummer kid they trot out occasionally. He's a great drummer for a three-year-old, which is to say not a great drummer. You know there is a sad back-story: only a spiteful ex-spouse buys a three-year-old kid drums.

The customers are just as good about wearing their farmers market costumes: wide-brimmed hats and sunglasses and tank tops and tented baby carriages and PBA-free water bottles and canvas NPR tote bags. Once my wife had to walk six blocks back to our car because she forgot and wore her bra.

And the dogs. Farmers market customers insist it is charming to bring along their pit bull to endure an hour on a hot summer sidewalk, drooling on the flip-flop feet of every sympathetic bystander. What comes out of my mouth is, "Can I say hi to your dog?" when I mean to say, "Mind if I rat you out to the Humane Society?"

I stroll from booth to booth, figuring one vendor might be a better farmer than the rest: fatter onions, greener kale, a better drawl, Key overalls. I get stressed when I can't tell a difference from one table to the next. I eventually go to whoever is closest to the exit. I buy a pound of kale and radishes, promising myself I'll eat healthy this week. When I get home I make room in the fridge by throwing away last week's kale and radishes.

The one thing truly local about our farmers markets is the way customers approach each booth politely, admiring the kiwi and leeks and whatever else doesn't grow in Nebraska, turning it over, asking a lot of questions ("What can you make with this?" "Is this gluten-free?"), engaging the vendor in a long discussion about the bio-ethnic, probiotic, organic yogurt they prefer, while their kid wipes a booger on the lettuce. Then they set it all back down and move politely to the next booth without buying anything.

It's not about the produce. It's a social occasion: a chance to stroll in the sun, mingle with lots of people, and feel a little better about ourselves. It's about trying to do the right thing, respecting our planet, and enjoying each other.

We're all in the market for that.

SOMETHING FISHY

My favorite place to go for seafood was a box of Mrs. Paul's. I love fish sticks. Throughout my life I thought I loved seafood. It turns out what I love is fried batter, tartar sauce and wine vinegar.

Tartar sauce is pickle relish in mayonnaise. It makes everything you put it on taste like a French hot dog. I buttered it over my little fish bricks like mortar.

At the tender age of thirteen[17] I discovered that fish doesn't always come in little golden Jenga blocks. This was revealed when I took a job as a busboy. In the traditional demonstration of freshness, the trout we served[18] had head and tail intact, an arching display like a canoe. Clearing tables, I didn't see much of the original fish — just the bones and leftover head, its eyes looking up at me in stunned surprise.

My mother once brought home an oily brown bag of dinner from Long John Silvers. Everything in it was brown. She fetched a bottle of wine vinegar which must have been in our house the whole time, but I had never seen it. Always practical, she probably bought the fish as an excuse to use up the vinegar.

Vinegar on breaded fish is delicious. With added tartar sauce, lovelier still. With enough tartar sauce and vinegar and deep-fat-fried

---

17 If there is anything tender about thirteen.
18 It was frozen.

batter I could eat shoelaces. I bet I could even like an oyster, which otherwise is as appetizing as a spoonful of snot.

There are sushi people and hot dog people, but it's an unnecessary division. Neither food tastes good by itself. With enough hot mustard or wasabi, you can hardly tell them apart.

The wasabi that local sushi restaurants serve isn't *real* wasabi. Real wasabi is very expensive and is used sparingly, mostly in Japan. We get green-dyed horseradish paste. I'm not complaining. When stirred with soy sauce, it creates the perfect condiment for sushi because it keeps it from tasting like sushi.

The first time I visited a sushi restaurant I played it safe and ordered a sampler platter. They brought me a colorful boat of little rice rolls, bits of salmon and tuna, jellyfish, and blobs with antennae and sucker feet. Everything was new to me. The first thing I popped into my mouth was the pretty green blob of wasabi. I learned that wasabi is a condiment, not a food. A very spicy condiment. The perfect amount of wasabi is enough to make your nose feel like it is going to pop off your face, but not so much that it actually does.

You mix your wasabi with soy sauce in a tiny dish. Sushi chefs don't pre-mix soy sauce and wasabi for you because it turns a taupish gray, the consistency of corpse drippings. Chefs prefer this to be your fault.

Take away the soy sauce, the wasabi, the wine vinegar and the tartar, and you're left with an authentic, super-healthy, high-protein, omega-3-fatty-acid mother lode of low-fat power food to invigorate your heart, brain and body. Sushi lowers the risk of depression, Alzheimer's and diabetes. This is the primary difference between sushi and hot dogs, which are basically a mash of cow lips, sphincters, and cancer-causing nitrates. Hot dogs spring from a fine German tradition of not wasting the things that by all rights you ought to waste.

The Japanese, on the other hand, invented "Krab" sticks, imitation crab meat formed from *surimi,* which is to say they made fish out of fish. That's like making cookies out of Oreos.

As an experiment, I ate sushi without the usual slather of condiments. Naked sushi has a slight floral smell and a buttery, fragile flavor. It is a little anti-climactic once you've discovered the thrill of a wasabi nose fire.

While researching this story I made a discovery: if you deep-fat-fry them, drizzle enough wine vinegar on them and smear them with tartar sauce, hot dogs taste just like fish sticks.

YOU ARE WHERE YOU EAT

You are what you eat, some say. That's fine, I get it: if you eat carrots, you feel good. If you eat a cheeseburger and waffle fries, you feel like a nap. If you eat gluten-free paleo tofu, you feel like a cave man, which is to say you want to club someone.

Want to play a game? If you're dining in my hometown of Omaha and you tell me what you're eating, I can tell you where you are. I'm like a tongue psychic. I'll prove it:

If you're picking wee bits of meat off a boar's head while a farmer, who still has the rest of the still-warm boar in the back of his pickup in the alley, sits at your table and tells you blissful tales of its former life ("He was a shy piglet, an orphan, but his aunt loved him and looked after him as if he were her own"):

You're at: The Boiler Room

If you're eating rabbit sautéed in duck fat after enjoying an appetizer so small it was brought to you on a spoon, but the real reason you're there is because the chef is so goddamn good-looking:

You're at: The Grey Plume

If you're eating a $45 steak:

You're at: Sullivan's

If you don't care because the bill is going on someone else's corporate credit card:
You're at: Omaha Prime

If you're filthy rich but you prefer a cheap steakhouse where every dish comes with a side of free spaghetti:
You're at: Piccolo Pete's

You're not filthy rich but you're politically connected:
You're at: Cascio's

You're neither, but you wish:
You're at: Venice Inn

If you're surrounded by autographed photos of famous people from the 1960s who once visited this room with ceiling beams shaped like a T-bone:
You're at: Johnny's Café

If you're eating macaroni and cheese made with a blend of five cheeses you've never heard of:
You're at: Marks Bistro

If the mac and cheese is bright orange and has hot dog chunks in it:
You're at: home, you're high, and you're eating out of the saucepan

If you're eating Mexican food in a restaurant where there aren't any Mexicans:
You're at: Cantina Laredo

If you're eating a cheeseburger at 11 PM surrounded by actors all yelling their stage stories at once:
You're at: Goldberg's

If it's 2 AM, you're drunk and you shout out the first thing you see on the menu:
You're at: Burger King's drive-thru

If you're eating ice cream with bits of fresh spinach and sage in it:
You're at: Ted & Wally's

If they offer to name the pint after you:
You're at: eCreamery

If you're drinking a gin and tonic that's brown and tastes like patchouli:
You're at: Lot 2

If it's brown and tastes like lemonade:
You're at: Side Door Lounge

If it's $3 and tastes like straight gin:
You're at: the Green Onion

It's $8 and tastes like straight tonic:
You're at: Harrah's Casino

If it's $3, you don't care how it tastes, you're just there to get laid:
You're at: The Interlude

If you waited twenty minutes for it because the bartender carved mountain spring ice into the shape of his own penis, then made you say please and thank you before he gave it to you:
You're at: The Berry & Rye

If you're drinking PBR while telling everyone around you that you were personal friends with Conor Oberst back in high school:
You're at: Pageturners Lounge

If you're drinking wine from a tap:
You're at: Brix

If you're drinking champagne from a tap:
You're at: The Homy Inn

If you're drinking sangria out of a pitcher:
You're at: España

If you're eating Italian food delivered by a waiter who insists on mispronouncing everything:
You're at: Spezia (which they pronounce "SPEE-zee-ah")

If he pronounces Italian perfectly even though he's from Sarajevo:
You're at: Avoli Osteria

If there are only two things on the menu but you took five minutes to decide which you wanted:
You're at: Amsterdam Falafel

If you're choosing between chicken fingers and fried mozzarella balls, Ranch dressing or honey-mustard dip, there are nostalgia signs on the wall, your server is wearing a red Oxford shirt with black pants and just finished group-singing a customized version of "Happy Birthday" that had the restaurant's name wedged into it:
You're at: someplace west of 84th Street. I'm sorry, but I can't be any more specific than that.

PARTY TIME

"OOOH, mints mints mints-mints-*mints!*" squealed the 40-ish woman in a frilly lavender dress. "I just *love* wedding mints! I can't stop eating them!"

That was the truth. She devoured all the sugary pink mints which had been carefully placed as party favors in front of her chair. Riding her sugar high, she moved on to another chair and ate those mints too, then continued from seat to seat like a locust until her sweater was dusted in sparkles and she shivered from joy and insulin overload.

"You can buy those at the grocery store," I offered. "Three dollars for a whole box of them."

"Oh, I know," she said, brushing me away with a flip of her hand. "But these are for weddings. You're not supposed to eat them by yourself."

She had a point. They're not called "TV Mints," or "Pink Sugar Frosted Mints." They're "Wedding Mints."

Mints are members of the food group we only eat at parties. These sugary, cream-cheesy mints — white, green and blood red — are often wrapped in gauzy twill and given away at Christmas to friends for whom we forgot to buy a real gift, and who will pass the frilly package on to someone else who will repeat the process until the mints have gathered too much travel lint to be re-giftable.

In contrast, we *squeee* with glee whenever we encounter those little cocktail weenies floating in a watery bath of diluted barbecue sauce, lukewarm in a candlelit chafing dish. Again, you're free to cook these at home. You could fill a cereal bowl full of them and park yourself in front of *Game of Thrones*, but you don't. Mini weenies are only for parties, presented in a stainless steel tub by a gaunt young caterer's assistant who's wearing a white button-down shirt and black vest with matching dyed hair who can't stop herself from saying, "I don't eat those. I'm vegan."

Same with those rolled up cream cheese tacos — *pinwheels,* they're called, even though they're so heavy Hurricane Andrew couldn't spin one. We sidle up to the party table, casually chatting while we eat one after another until we've consumed a brick's worth of cream cheese while saying, "Oh, no, I'm not hungry. I'll just pick."

Where else but at a wedding do you eat mixed nuts with a spoon?

Where else but at a party do you see M&Ms in popcorn? Or cheeseburgers so tiny you could tuck one into your shirt pocket?

Do you make punch at home? Of course you don't, because you care about what you drink. But for a party you'll mix Popov vodka with two cans of plain-label canned fruit juice and a two-liter bottle of store-label Sprite and get fifteen people drunk for $8. There's something about ladling pink mystery booze into a Solo cup that says, "Party!"

You know why we get excited about little ham salad sandwiches cut into white-bread circles? Because that's exactly how we wanted to eat them when we were six years old. "Mom, would you please cut the crust off my baloney and cheese sandwich?"

"No. The crust is the best part. It's good for you. Eat it." Get married, and your mom will prepare a whole tray of hand-carved, crustless little Wonder bread masterpieces just to taunt your new bride. We see those at a party and our inner child leaps in our belly like baby John the Baptist.

From the host's point of view, parties are a perfect opportunity to go all out with your kitchen experiments. Our New Year's Eve menu last year started with six bricks of butter, a pound of pastry dough, various unpronounceable cheeses, and cured meats made from only the finest ears and lips. If the calories and salt don't kill you, a cocktail toothpick stuck in your throat will.

We don't eat like that every day because we don't want to die just yet. But apparently we don't care whether *your* new year starts with a heart attack on January 1.

Fact: we look skinnier if you look fatter. Have another cream-puff?

WE'RE DOOMED. SO WHAT'S FOR DINNER?

Global warming. Underwear bombers. Gluten. Life feels precarious these days. I've gone beyond worrying about tomorrow to worrying whether I'll make it to happy hour.

To console myself, I make every meal a Last Supper. Not the broken bread and bloody wine kind, but real comfort food that will send me to the Pearly Gates with a happy belly.

SHOW ME THE FAT

The foundation of all comfort food is fat. Lard, oil, and butter all trigger our evolutionary dopamine, signaling, "Everything is fine. Go back to sleep." Fat feels safe. Fat = not starving. Fat is mother's milk. Boobs are made of fat.

Skinny people make great models because they look like clothes hangers. But when you need real comforting, nobody wants a bony hug. We want to be wrapped in soft, cozy fat.

Cheese, the refined offspring of fat, is happiness shaped like a brick. Cheese needs no cooking, so guys like it. When it melts, it turns into gravy. Cheese is fat you can hold in your hands. It's stackable fat. Without cheese, nachos are nothing more than corn chip and hamburger salad.

MAC & CHEESE, PLEASE

Macaroni is a benign carrier food, like white bread: flavorless, with just enough structure to hold the food you really want to be eating. Mac and cheese is a go-to comfort food because it's made almost entirely of cheese. The macaroni is there only so you can pick up the cheese. That's why it's shaped like a handle.

Macaroni and cheese is comforting for another reason: your mom made it for you. It harkens back to a time when you were clothed, housed and fed by a servant.

Kraft tries to capitalize on our pathetic loneliness by putting mac and cheese in a do-it-yourself box, but nothing is more loveless than pouring powdered cheese onto skinny noodles for yourself. Kraft macaroni and cheese tastes like parents too busy for their kids.

What goes with mac and cheese? Ketchup and regret.

A DUO FOR WHEN YOU'RE SOLO

The comfort food that's okay to make for myself: grilled cheese sandwiches and tomato soup. It's especially good when you're sick. Here's my recipe:

1. Butter two slices of toothy wheat bread.
2. Butter the pan.
3. Butter the butter.
4. Smear yogurt on the inside of the bread slices. Do not use nonfat yogurt. This is a grilled cheese friggin' sandwich, for Pete's sake.
5. Lay on some sharp cheddar cheese and dust lightly with cayenne pepper.

If you are expecting nuclear obliteration or fire-and-brimstone, add a bit more cayenne. It will help you acclimate.

My recipe for tomato soup:

1. Open the can.

CHEDDAR IS BETTER

I love to wrap my arms and legs around a giant bowl of popcorn, with a side of cheddar cheese and wine. Wine, cheese and popcorn are a holy trinity, and it tastes even better wearing my flannel jammies.[19]

If you don't have any servants, you may find some comfort in convenience store microwave burritos. They are as fun to peel as a banana, without tasting like one. There is enough fat and salt in a burrito to kill you mercifully before you die of whatever cataclysm made you want a burrito in the first place.

Ice cream is nobody's comfort food, really. We keep dipping into it only because it looks so comforting when Meg Ryan eats it in, well, every Meg Ryan movie.

BREAKFAST FOR DINNER

Comfort Food #3: breakfast for dinner. I don't know why this works except that the breakfast foods we prefer are Froot Loops, pancakes and bacon, which is to say, candy. The reverse doesn't work as well: nobody is comforted by roast beef and mashed potatoes for breakfast.

Maybe the world isn't really coming to an end. I know I can't eat comfort food every meal just to feel safe. But when I'm feeling insecure, it seems smart to stock up on comfort food, just in case.

That's what the survivalists do.

---

[19] How popcorn got into my flannel jammies, I'll never know.

BLOW ME AWAY

The first time I witnessed a real breakthrough in the culinary arts was when a fistful of Pop Rocks exploded in my mouth. Not as in, "exploding with flavor!" As in, they blew up.

"Taste the Explosion!" the packaging exclaimed. I knew what an explosion tasted like, because when I was eleven years old a firecracker went off in my mouth.

Because I did not learn a thing from that episode, I opened my mouth and tossed in a handful of jewel-red Pop Rocks. Like every other kid trying Pop Rocks for the first time, I screamed and spit out the crackling carnage, panicking at the sight of my foamy, blood-colored spit. Then, like every other kid, I exclaimed, "Cool!"

Cereal makers lead the creative charge for kids, turning honeycombs, s'mores and doughnuts into corn-based, primary-colored breakfast that goes down like a spoonful of sugar. But finding more ways to eat sugar isn't exactly a breakthrough.

For grown-ups, behold the *booze asmooch*... the *amused douche*... [pause while I look it up]... the *amuse-bouche*, a one-bite treat brought to your table by the chef in frillier restaurants. This delicacy is his calling card, meant to sum up his entire philosophy in a single spoonful of raw salmon or mint foam. The *amuse-bouche* is technically not an appetizer because it comes before the appetizers and you didn't order it. It's more a thing to admire than a thing to eat.

I eat it anyway. The last one I had tasted like Thanksgiving dinner and dessert all in one bite.

If anyone is watching, it's polite to roll your eyes around thoughtfully as you ponder its slimy, slippery texture. *How bold! Bravo!* If nobody's watching, you can use your napkin to wipe off your tongue.

The urge for creativity has invaded instant coffee, starting with adding cheap powdered styrofoam that looks quite like you actually paid $5 for a cappuccino. No more plain powdered non-diary creamer.[20] Now you can enjoy additives like Coffee-mate Belgian Chocolate Toffee, Parisian Almond Crème (you know it's really French because it has the accent), or Crème Brûlée. *(Three different accents! And no, I'm not making these up.)* How about Tiramisu Cheesecake? (Okay, I made that one up just to see if I could. Good, huh?) These powdered miracles are for people who don't like real coffee but like holding cups.

The real food innovation of the last decade is in packaging. To make a no-drip ketchup bottle, Heinz developed a tiny sphincter spout that doesn't leak at all until you squeeze the bottle hard enough until it bursts like a zit across your hot dog, across the table, up the mink coat of the woman at the next booth, then onto the hairy hand of her very serious, very burly date.[21] Heinz needs to solve the squeeze bottle's tendency to sound like a fart, which inevitably happens within earshot of 8-year-old boys who giggle and repeat that sound for the rest of the day until you send them to bed early.

Frito-Lay has perfected an exploding potato chip bag that tears open everywhere except along the seam labeled "Open here."

---

20 If it's powdered and non-dairy, is it still creamer?
21 Does that example seem a little specific? Wel, yeah, I did that. Really, though, didn't she ask for it by wearing a mink coat to McDonald's?

OF MICE AND ME

Nature's Harvest reduces waste by putting only 3 ounces of granola in their 16-ounce box, cradled in a little biodegradable plastic bag surrounded by a box of, I presume, fresh 100% organic country air. This reduces our use of biofuels by making the delivery truck lighter.

The age-old wax-and-cardboard milk carton now has a plastic spout on top, right next to the original spout. Convenient! Just 1) unscrew the lid, then 2) break out the "freshness seal" underneath by pulling the attached plastic ring which 3) breaks off, then 4) dig out the damn thing by stabbing it with a screwdriver, which works so well milk squirts up your nose, which feels/smells oddly familiar because your brother once made you laugh too hard at the breakfast table when you were seven. This innovation takes three times longer and drips twice as much as the original fold-open spout no one remembers how to use.

Food trend-setters: if you want to innovate but are short of inspiration, here are three suggestions:

1. create cling wrap that sticks to something besides itself
2. edible biscotti-flavored coffee cups
3. grocery store tomatoes that taste like a tomato

While I'm waiting, pass me some more of that exploding food.

CONDIMENTARY, MY DEAR WATSON

I was 27 years old when I learned that ketchup isn't automatically included with a refrigerator. Every fridge I ever saw had ketchup, mustard and pickles in it. I never met anyone who bought ketchup.

My formative years were spent living with a series of women, starting with my mother. I was encouraged to do "boy things" like mow grass, lift furniture and stick my arm into the toilet up to my shoulder to retrieve a lost phone or contact lens. I did not have security clearance to help with refrigerator inventory.

When I was newly divorced, I became the first tenant in a freshly renovated apartment, complete with brand new appliances. I opened the refrigerator to a scene from *2001: A Space Odyssey*. I blinked as the bright light poured out from the gleaming white plastic and chrome, without a hint of humanity. I pulled out a note pad and wrote across the top: "Grocery List," and I underlined it. Beneath that I wrote: "Everything."

At the grocery store I learned that cinnamon, rosemary and cayenne are about the same price as silver. I needed all the basics: glassware, flour, sugar, measuring cups, a can opener, mixing bowls, a corkscrew, and ketchup. I looked around for the financing department.

I learned that "ketchup" is not a brand name. I found a variety of bottle sizes and shapes, but I figured it didn't matter because the contents were the identical tempera-paint red. I chose Heinz because "Heinz Ketchup" sounded familiar. I selected a tub of Plochman's mustard because it came in a familiar yellow plastic barrel with a red nipple on top, like the one from which I nursed mustard as a kid. Heinz made mustard too, but "Heinz Mustard" didn't sound right.

A new refrigerator with a fresh bottle of mustard and ketchup is a glorious site, clean as an operating room, sleek as an IKEA showroom. My apartment was now a home.

Mustard comes in many varieties: spicy, brown, sweet, flecked with brown bits of what look like bugs but I think are seeds. There is *Dijon,* which is French for "costs twice as much."

These are gourmet foods, not condiments. You can tell the difference because the fancy mustards go on the top shelf of the refrigerator with your capers, feta cheese and cocktail onions. The yellow barrel of regular mustard goes in the door next to the ketchup.

Ketchup takes up a whole section at the grocery store. Family size, picnic-size, upside-down bottle with no-drip spout. But the stuff inside is all just ketchup. Some try labeling it "catsup," which makes my pinky itch to stick out. "Catsup" sounds like dinner's ready at a Vietnamese restaurant. I don't see any hot and spicy ketchup, smoked pineapple mango ketchup, or extra chunky ketchup. The Heinz guys are smacking their foreheads right now for not thinking of it, and while they were making fancy upside-down bottles with clever slogans, the Mexicans invented hot and spicy chunky ketchup which they named *salsa,* now the most popular condiment in the fridge.

So how did ketchup earn a place in every American kitchen? We don't put ketchup on chicken, pizza or tacos. The bottle in my refrigerator today is the same one I bought in 1987, having outlived three refrigerators. Thanks to the magic of the American food industry, it's still good. I've been through 200 bottles of Ranch dressing, which I put on everything from chips to chicken wings to cheeseburgers — just about everything but salads — but Ranch is still considered a second-tier condiment. I recently encountered Ranch-flavored Doritos, a sure a sign of its ubiquity. There are no ketchup-flavored chips. You don't see Hint of Ketchup Triscuits.

Yet ketchup is part of our religious ritual. Your burger arrives. You open it, lift off the bun cap and pick off the lettuce like a wet napkin. *Shake-shake-shake* of salt, *shook-shook-shook* of pepper. Squeeze a spiral of ketchup followed by a zig-zag of mustard. Every restaurant table is stocked with four items. You know what they are. Since we all agree mustard, ketchup, salt and pepper are supposed to be on the burger, why doesn't the chef add it for you with his masterful hand, fancy as a $5 cappuccino? Because he knows you'll do it too, without looking, without tasting, and then you'll ruin it.

The only other restaurant food I know of that is delivered to your table unfinished is pancakes. That's because restaurants give you a dozen different syrups to distract you from your hangover.

I've shopped for refrigerators. When I visit Massive Appliance Mart, the dazzling array of crisper trays, French door options and water dispensers is overwhelming. What I'm looking for is a white refrigerator that comes with a stop-sign-red bottle of ketchup and a PlaySkool-yellow tub of mustard already in the door tray. Sold!

THE BOXER

Boxed wine used to be the booze equivalent of "cheese food product." What it lacked in edibility, it made up for in volume.

There has been an ongoing evolution in wine packaging. First, they started wrapping bottles in jute netting, to show how fancy they were. Then they tried getting rid of the cork, offering a whitewash of disparate reasons:

1. "Cork is natural. Harvesting natural things is bad for the environment."
2. "Plastic corks are more stable and protect wine better."
3. "Screw tops create less waste and provide a better seal."

First, cork is not a living thing. It is the by-product of a living thing. Trees miss their cork like my cat misses the hair on the couch.

Plastic corks are indeed more stable: they can survive in a landfill for 20,000 years. They make wine taste like plastic corks.

Screw tops are sensible, except that they are forever linked to Boone's Farm Country Kwencher. I liked Country Kwencher just fine as a kid, although even then I was bothered by the spelling. If you are marketing to hicks, why not go all the way: *Kuntry Kwencher?*[22] You'll find Boone's Farm proudly displayed in convenience stores that don't sell wine, which is an ominous give-away: although it is

---

22 Okay, I see why.

in a wine bottle, Boone's Farm is not wine. It is a "malt-based beverage," which is to say it is wine-flavored beer. This is the poster child of screw-top bottles.

Wine *connoisseurs* claim they can tell by the taste of a wine the region from which the screw cap was mined. This distinct taste is referred to as *ferroir*.

Yes, corks go bad. Yes, cork failure will spoil expensive wines. Yes, they often crumble into the bottle. Or break in half, leaving an irretrievable plug you have to push into the bottle with a screwdriver. That is part of the mystique. If everyone could open a wine bottle, what would be the fun of being a snob? The pageantry and fussy corkscrew finesse are part of the fun, despite the gnawing awareness that it would be more easily accomplished with safety goggles and a cordless drill.

A cork gives clues as to what pleasure (or not) is to come. You don't need to sniff the cork like they do in the movies. Just look at it. Is it moldy? Is there foul gunk on the end that is nowhere near a wine color? This is not esoteric. You use the same trick with bread: if it is green and covered with fur, you don't need to sniff it.[23]

Today, box wine presents tempting advantages. First, it gives you four bottles of wine for the price of — and in the space of — three. What comes out of the box tastes very much like wine. There is no cork or screw top to intimidate you. There is no top at all. This brings me to my favorite part about box wine: it comes out of a spigot. Wine on tap.

The empty package is cardboard, which is more recyclable than glass. Although the bladder bag inside a box of wine looks like a worn-out spleen, it is recyclable too. They claim this collapsible bag helps wine last longer, since no air gets in while you drain it. Air is the

---

23 Cheese is the opposite. The more green fur, the better. Perhaps this is why it goes well with wine.

enemy of wine. This is a useful tip for those mythical people who don't finish a bottle once they open it.

As I remove the plastic bladder and notice how much wine is still clinging to its wrinkly folds, my Scottish roots compel me to wring it out, which is about as classy a maneuver as wringing a placenta. But the result is an extra half glass of wine, which I consider my reward for bothering to recycle.

The only downside to box wine is that, like the giant 12-pack of toilet paper, it is embarrassing to unload at the check-out lane. But once you get it home, it sits neatly on a shelf, ready to dispense at the touch of your finger. And if snobby friends come over, just empty its bladder into that decanter you never use.

DON'T BE SUCH A SQUARE

I had my heart set on making pizza, but discovered I didn't have any yeast. So I saved time by buying one of those dough-in-a-tube products. I cracked open the tube and unrolled the yellow dough. It was the shape of a cookie sheet.

I don't know if that shape is supposed to be convenient for me or for them, but I didn't want a rectangular pizza. I don't like how rectangles taste. If God wanted pizza to be rectangular, he would have shaped Italy like Wyoming. I associate rectangular pizza with Roy's Pizza in my old home town. Roy's Pizza was made with boiled hamburger.

So I wadded the dough into a ball, mushed it up a little bit, then stretched and pulled it out into a...*rectangle?* Let's try again.

I balled it up again and whacked it with my rolling pin, then rolled it out again.

Rectangle.

No matter what I did, the dough would return to its original dimensions, as if it had a geometric memory, as if the shape were a Pillsbury trademark.

Any other time I'd be proud to be able to roll a sphere of dough into perfect corners. When I need to roll a rectangle, I usually get an amoeba. It's nearly impossible, but here I was, so good at it I couldn't *stop* doing it.

I got frustrated. I didn't want no skanky Roy-ass rectangle pizza.

Laura touched my shoulder gently as if it were a mousetrap and whispered, "Michael, relax. Deep breath. Count to ten. Cooking is fun."

It is only the second time in my life that I have actually counted to ten. The other time was also in the kitchen.

I whacked, kneaded, wheedled, stretched and rolled, to a draw. It was certainly not a circle, and one might see hints of a parallelogram, but the finished shape was mostly blobic. Laura thought it looked like a slug. But at least it was not a rectangle.

The overworked crust turned out as light and flaky as slap leather. It tasted rectangular.

This morning I lifted my head from my rectangular pillow, rose from my rectangular bed, shuffled out of my rectangular bedroom and saw my rectangular morning hair in my rectangular bathroom mirror. I had eaten a rectangle, and now I felt like I was becoming one, like the guy in T*he Fly*.

As I write this I notice that my computer looks quite like a rectangle rising triumphantly out of a round ball of dough.

OUT OF THE MOLD

Before the dawn of refrigerators, back when humans made ice cubes by banging chunks of glacier against their foreheads, leftover food storage options were simpler. You either: 1) ate it, 2) it rotted, or 3) it rotted and you ate it anyway.

#3 is how we discovered cheese.

Today milk comes in handy take-home jugs, so it's hard to remember that at one time the jugs were made of leather and were attached to cows. The next time you are at the grocery store dairy aisle and you open the cooler door to the bright white array of milk options, try to imagine a row of fuzzy pink teats instead.

It is no longer our instinct to reach between a half-ton animal's legs, grabbing whatever dangles there and squirting what comes out into our mouths. It was a dicey idea even then. Drinking cow milk probably started, as most things do, as a fraternity prank. "I dare you drink that, Og. Go on! What you — chicken?"

"Og no chicken!" Og reply, shaking hairy fist. "Og show you!" Og grab teat, Og narrowly avoid hoof to flat forehead. Og win bet. Hey — Og like milk! Milk good! Surprise! Og famous.

Not long after Og learned we could drink cow's milk, some kid squeezed himself more than he could finish. His mother yelled, "Cows don't grow on trees, y'know," which the kid was pretty sure he did know. He couldn't put the leftover milk in the refrigerator because it hadn't been invented yet, and it took the boy only one kick in the forehead to learn he couldn't put it back in the cow.

So his half-full glass of milk sat on the counter, where it fermented, festered and foamed, until vein-blue tentacles of mold crawled out of it. One day, by some quirk of fate, a little bit of rennet drooled into the mix. Rennet is a nice word for stomach mucus. It is beyond me to guess how stomach fluid got into his milk, but remember we're talking about a preteen boy. The mother, to get rid of the growing stink, moved the festering blob of coagulating milk-fur into a nearby cave, where it proceeded to rot.

The furry milk continued to clot in the cave. In a fit of starvation — or upon another frat-boy dare — someone took a bite. To everyone's astonishment, he did not die.

In those days, any food that you could leave out for weeks and still eat was a big deal. Just ask the guys who invented Twinkies. Nonetheless, furry, rotten food is hard to sell, something Og learned when he tried to market his invention.

The live mold that makes bleu cheese blue is *brevibacterium livens,* the same bacteria that makes your feet stink, which should come as no surprise. Og couldn't call his new invention "toe cheese" because that name was already taken. He went with "bleu cheese" because food seems fancier when it stinks in French.

Sauerkraut was discovered pretty much the same way as cheese. There was always a lot of leftover cabbage, because it's made of cabbage. Like the bleu cheese, it sat and fermented in its own gank until someone got so hungry that he took a bite and decided it tasted better than starvation. Because Germans name things literally — *volks wagen* = family car, *sauer kraut* = rotten cabbage — it grew popular only among the Germans. The rest of us might have tried sauerkraut sooner had they named it *bleu chou.*

The importance of attractive food labeling is especially evident in Korea, where traditional *dim sum* delicacies include "White Cloud Phoenix Talons," which don't sell as well when you call them by their German name, "Little Steamed Chicken Toenails." One exception is the recent rise in yogurt sales, with the fanciest brands bragging about having "live, active cultures!" So far this has only worked with yogurt, a food we already expect to be bad. The beef industry, in comparison, has yet to figure out how to sell meat "with live, active bacteria!"

Today, Americans prefer their food mold-free and bleached white. Pasteurized, wrapped in tamper-proof safety foil, vacuum-sealed, boxed, shrink-wrapped and refrigerated, American Cheese is aptly named. We like the packaging of American Cheese because it keeps the mold out. The French like the packaging of American Cheese because it keeps the cheese in.

I was sipping red wine one afternoon at my favorite French hangout when the UPS man clomped in and delivered a slatted wooden crate with what appeared to be a raccoon inside. Rachel the Ever-Surly Bartender lit up with a squeal: "The bleu cheese is here!" The Frisbee-sized wheel of cheese arrived unwrapped, unrefrigerated, and covered in a haze of blue-gray. Rachel reached right through the slats, pulled off a chunk and popped it into her mouth, fuzz and all. "It's so good when it's fresh!"

Fresh?

Even Og no eat that.

FOR GOOD MEASURE

Recipes used to be simple:

1. *Hit bird with rock*
2. *Pull off feathers*
3. *Hold over fire until black and crunchy*

Next came the invention of tools. Cave-man cooks, sensitive because up until then they had done nothing but burn things over a fire, decided they would get more respect if they re-named every tool specifically for cooking. Pokey sticks became *utensils*.

After they invented the arrow, the knife and the alphabet, things moved quickly. Food could be cut into smaller and smaller bits until it became too little to hold. This fostered the invention of bowls, mixers and measuring spoons to assemble the bits back together into something manageable. Instructions were called *recipes*. Cooks became *chefs*.

How can you screw up something as simple as a spoon? When a recipe calls for a tablespoon of ground pigeon flakes, you can't use a spoon off the table, because a *table* spoon holds only a teaspoon. How much does a *tea* spoon hold? Who knows? Even the British don't use tea spoons. They stir tea with a *demi-spoon,* which, despite its name, is not half a spoon. That soup spoon nobody uses holds a tablespoon.

Heaping teaspoon: two words nobody thought would be paired together. A teaspoon is not your tool if you want to make a heap.

Does a drinking cup hold a cup of liquid? Of course not. It holds 1.5 cups. If I cup my hands I can carry 1/8 of a cup. A cup holds 8 ounces of flour, which weighs 4 ounces. This is why we throw up our hands and go to Burger King.

Heaven forbid we use the metric system like the rest of the post-Cro-Magnon world. You know you are on shaky ground when your only compatriots using cups, pints and quarts are the British, who should not be trusted with food or naming things. The British call a spatula a *scoop*. The Scots call it a *tosser*, but that's forgivable: if your homeland was famous for haggis you'd toss your food too.

Then consider the indistinct measurements, like a *pinch* and a *dash*. Not precise, but they use our fingers, which we always have handy.

We can do better. How about a hand of thyme? A finger of cake frosting? A nose of Coke? Remember the Super Bowl when Justin Timberlake introduced a cup of Janet Jackson?

Care for a glom of yogurt? A swipe of peanut butter? I know you can get a schmear of cream cheese, but I always feel a little cheated. No wonder: I looked up "schmear" and the word translates as "corrupt."

I love coffee because I grind the coffee beans in a coffee grinder, put them in a coffee maker and make coffee in a coffee cup. I appreciate such clarity first thing in the morning.

But not too much clarity. Do we really need to call it a *frying* pan?

In my kitchen I have a whisk, which is used for mixing. My mixer uses beaters. I beat with a tenderizer, which mashes, but to mash potatoes I use a ricer, and I cook rice in the steamer while I steam vegetables in the colander before I toss them into a salad with dressing I whip with my whisk.

My blender has buttons for *chop, grate, crumb, purée, liquefy* and *whip*. Guess what it doesn't have a button for.

YOU ANIMAL

OF MICE AND ME

Through my high school years I worked at a motel doing all their laundry. Every day I washed every sheet from every bed. I was a master sheet folder, and my reward for speed was to have a few minutes between each load to do absolutely nothing but watch the huge dryer drums go 'round. It was all the entertainment my busy 16-year-old brain needed.

Around sunset, when all the maids, maintenance staff and managers had gone home, I could lock the door to the laundry room and have the place to myself — sort of. There was a big hole in the wall that had once been a window, now just a portal between my space and the recently added garage. The empty window ledge was now a viewing platform for the motel mice. Three or four would come out of the wall each evening and rest their pointy chins on their rice-thin forearms, their tiny black eyes, small and dark as poppy seeds, watching me work. It was their happy hour.

It was unsettling at first, but I grew glad to have company. The mice didn't judge my work and wouldn't interrupt as I told them stories. I didn't try to hug 'em and pet 'em and squeeze 'em. When I was finished I would look up to say good-night, but they were already gone, off to their own jobs.

They worked hard through the night. A motel is a lot of territory to cover.

Every morning the manager would arrive ranting about the "infestation." He would enlist me to help brainstorm on mousetrap design and placement. I love gadgets, so I enjoyed devising clever systems to entrap tiny intruders, using their insatiable greed against them. After the manager left, I would make my rounds, tripping all the traps, leaving the cheese and peanut butter booty for my mini-uns.

My affection for mice sparked when I was thirteen. The pet store had a sale on mice: one for a dollar. I had a dollar. I asked my mother if I could have a mouse, that I'd pay for it myself and feed it and care for it and…"

"No."

I bought one anyway. I named him Henry as I carried him home, hidden in a little box in my coat. That was as far my plan went. I slunk up to my room and, having neglected to consider where I might keep him, dropped him into my empty wastebasket, a metal cylinder brightly painted to look like a giant can of Pabst Blue Ribbon.

Immediately the mouse began leaping to unimaginable heights, out of the can like popcorn, and I slammed a book over it to contain him. The book didn't quite cover the hole, so I flipped the whole can over. It worked until nightfall, when the mouse began leaping again, now smashing his tiny head into the bottom — top? — of the can like a steel drum. Mortified that my mother would hear, I flipped it back with the book on top and added a blanket to muffle the thumps.

By morning Henry the mouse was dead of a broken neck. I never felt worse about myself than I did at that moment: selfish, dishonest, and cruel. Since then I have viewed mice with an affection and tenderness born of guilt, as if the death of Henry the Christ saved the lives of many mice after him, whose sins have been forgiven.

The closest I came to having another mouse was in college. I took a class in Experimental Psychology, training with the other students in the scientific method. We were issued a chart, a cage with a lever, and a rat.

The Charles River rat is not so named because it thrives along the Charles River, but because they come from the Charles River Rat Factory, a business that supplies rats specifically prepared — or more accurately, specifically unprepared — for experiments. They are pure, as white as innocence, with round eyes red as candy. Once each rat has been used for a single experiment, he cannot be used for another because, having learned a thing or two, he is now considered tainted. I didn't ask, but I presume they were recycled to Biology 101.

As I worked with my rat, whose cage was in the middle of all the other neat columns of stacked rats, I daydreamed of setting them all free. But I was tainted too, resigned that it wouldn't change anything. I got an A.

Every morning the motel manager would wander into the laundry room whistling, or perhaps singing outright, his tenor voice a gift to man and mouse. He was a deeply spiritual person, young and full of sunny optimism. At the sight of the flipped, empty traps he would stop mid-*"hallelu..."* and go silent. A Yosemite Sam fury invaded him.

His religion didn't allow dancing, much less cursing. He didn't condone using a substitute word for a swear word, like *jeepers bucking cripes,* because that was just swearing without conviction. Stomping and flailing were dangerously close to dancing, so in the end he was rendered inanimate but for his bulging veins, quivering pupils and pressure-cooker lava. The quietest quiet falls when you are expecting an explosion and don't get it.

To this day he doesn't know I was complicit. He never will. He died at the age of thirty-three, an otherwise lucky number. He was a motocross racer, and his bike had come apart. There were rumors of tampering, but I all I know is that he stored his motorcycle in the garage, next to my laundry room, surrounded by mousetraps.

LE BARK

I'm learning a new language.

I worked hard at Spanish. I learned a lot of words. But Spaniards speak in such a machine-gun monotone that no matter what they say, I respond with, "*¿Excúse me?*"

Italian is much easier. The words are about the same as Spanish, so I had a head start. Real Italians all speak as clearly as the people on the *Beginner's Italian* recordings. Unlike the Spanish, they don't automatically hate me for being American.

I like to be good at things. If I'm not immediately darling at something, I usually give it up. I don't even bother to try any of the languages where the letters are upside down and backwards, the sentences read the wrong way, or they draw words using a branch.

I have two cats. Cat language is a snap to learn. Basically, there are only two phrases:

1. *"Row-WOWW"* = "Be a good chap and open me a can of Friskie Delights Sardine Pâté, would you?"

2. *Blank stare* = "You bore me."

With those two phrases, my cats and I understand each other pretty well.

I am caring for my girlfriend's dog Phooey for a few days, and I am getting an immersion course in Dog. I already speak a little Dog, from my days working at the Humane Society. I once stopped by the kennel of a particularly beautiful Australian shepherd, considered among the brightest of breeds. He lifted my hand with his elegant snout and tossed it onto his sweet head as if to say, "Scritch it?" I did, and he was pleased. He repeated the motion, guiding my hand atop his head with his nose. I skritched again. "Very good," he said with his eyes. Then he lifted my hand a third time, but set it on the cage door latch. His eyes said, "Got it?"

The trouble I'm having is that Phooey is not an Australian shepherd, but a purebred Shih Tzu. Not only is his vocabulary much smaller, but he was bred in one of those countries that writes with sticks.

Here is what I have translated so far:

1. *Jumps up against my shin, dances, spins on the floor and pants* = "I must go potty." "Let's do tricks!" "Walkies!" "We're going driving!" Pretty much anything seems to be the right answer.

2. *Low grumble, then sneezes on me* = "I am not getting through to you!" He never gets through to me. By some quirk of evolution, he never runs out of snot.

When Italians speak with foreigners, they continue in Italian as if you understand them. They presume that the beautiful sound of their language will carry the meaning well enough, like music. Americans reply with either "Gratzee" or "Skoozee."

The Spanish look at you with an expression that conveys, *Why did you even bother to come here, if you can't speak our language?* Then they speak to you in English that is better than yours.

The French will say, equally well in French or English, "I don't want to talk to you. Go away."

OF MICE AND ME

When Americans talk to foreigners, we TALK LOU-DER AND SLOW-ER WITH MORE DICK-SHUN, as if the listener were equal parts deaf and retarded.

Phooey and I are currently at a standstill, each of us looking at the other, tilting our heads left, then right. Normally, I like to communicate with animals, but I suspect that if I learn the Shih Tzu dialect, I'll end up leading the life of a beleaguered hairdresser slave.

ROUTINE MAINTENANCE

It's freezing. I drag myself out of my warm bed. The dog stays behind. He used to pounce whenever I budged, following my every motion as if I were made of bacon. By now he has figured out I'm just going to the bathroom and that I'll return shortly to get dressed. He knows he's wasting his energy until I venture downstairs, whereupon he'll circle my feet like attacking Sioux.

I have become so predictable that the dog and my cats know everything I'm about to do. As I shuffle barefoot into the kitchen, my cat Spek is already there looking bored, even though she's only been there fifteen seconds. She knows she'll be fed a moist pâté of ground fish guts out of a can within the next three minutes. She begins to meow at 1 minute 30 seconds out of habit, knowing it won't speed me up any. The dog stands guard, having learned the hard way that the cat bowl is off limits, but anything that touches the floor is fair game.

The animals weave between my clumsy feet with the agility of egrets picking food from a hippo's mouth. Their safety requires that they know exactly where I'm going to step next. They do.

People say days go by faster as you get older. I know at least one person who is certain that time literally *is* going faster, and although he says it with scientific authority, his theory still smells as if freshly pulled out of his ass.

I believe it isn't going faster, it's just that as we get older we become more routine. It gets harder to distinguish one day from the next, and they begin to blur together into one representative experience. You remember a year as if it were a day, because every day that year was pretty much the same.

When you're a kid, every day is unique. Your brain is an empty jar. As you age you start developing preferences, then favorites, and soon your favorite things start to congeal into habits, then cement into routines. If my newspaper isn't delivered, I can't eat breakfast.

The last unique, remarkable day may have been months ago. "Why, it seems like 4th of July was just last week!" When days are identical, your brain condenses them into one just to preserve memory space.

I had lunch with a friend who was about to get a new tattoo.

"Of what?" I asked.

"I don't know."

He's not new to this. He already looks like an ad for the tattoo parlor.

"You're getting a tattoo that will last your whole life, and you haven't made up your mind yet?"

"I had some space to fill."

As tattoos go, I am a blank slate. I can't commit to anything, out of fear I might change my mind later. Even the classic "Momma" is chancy — she could turn on me any day. Maybe she was just being nice all this time because I was little and she felt sorry for me, and now she's just waiting until I'm old enough to tell me what a pain in the ass I was.

"Each tattoo reminds me where my life was at the time I got it," my friend explained. "It's not the design itself that's important, but the memory it stirs up." He is a walking scrapbook of unconnected imagery: a wagon wheel, an eagle, a guitar. I decide not to quiz him on the sheriff's badge.

To shake up my life I try to do something unique every day. Maybe I'll get a tattoo when I'm 90, when there's not enough time left to change my mind about it.

I cringe when people get engaged on Christmas, or whose birthdays fall on New Year's Eve. I know I'd forget one event or the other. When I plan a celebratory occasion like an engagement or wedding, I'll look at the calendar and pick the longest stretch of time between two existing holidays, and stick the new event right in the middle. My goal: when I'm 90 years old, every day will be something to celebrate, something unique, and time will stand still.

PET PEEVE

I grew up with a little black dog. I don't know what kind she was, and I don't care. She wasn't *my* dog — she was part of the family before I was, and she always looked at me as if to say, "Who let *you* in?"

Her name was Eenie, as in "Meenie Minie Moe," the names of her siblings.

Eenie was old. Her fur was stiff and wiry, not nice to pet, and she wouldn't let you anyway. She growled and snapped at me. When I learned that you could call female dogs bitches and not get grounded, I called her that at every opportunity.

As happens with pets when you are young, one day she was gone. No fuss, no explanation. My four older brothers and sisters did not keep me apprised of every family event — maybe they were crushed and I didn't notice — but I suspect that she was "sent to live at a farm." I was too embarrassed to ask, because I didn't know how much time had passed before I noticed she was missing.

When I thought the appropriate amount of time had passed — about a day — I began begging for a puppy. Every day for years I supplicated, regular as a morning yawn. Once my dad brought home a guppy and said it was mine. Was that word play, on "puppy?" It was one of those ugly black ones with spherical bug eyes on either side of its head. He put it in our big aquarium with the other guppies. "You can feed it," he offered.

"Can I walk it?" I replied.

He just walked away, as if *I* were the weird one.

You can't hug a goldfish. You can't hug a turtle or a snake — and no, boa constrictor hugs don't count.

A few years later — I might have been twelve years old — I was sitting in the bathtub, quietly crying to myself. Looking down at my pale belly bulging out from a big dinner, I was afraid I would grow up to be fat. (Wasted tears: three years later I was 6 feet 2 inches tall and 125 pounds.) The door to the bathroom creaked open and I shrieked, "I'm in here!" That was our standard response to the other seven members of the household who might be wanting to use the only bathroom.

We were not one of those families that walked around naked in front of each other. Indeed, I hadn't seen anything between my mother's chin and knees since I was breastfed. But the door opened farther, and terrified I protested again in falsetto, *"I'm in here!"*

A three-month-old Labrador puppy crept in. He was more fuzz than fur, fat and round with a pointy rat tail that stuck up like an antenna as he sniffed around.

My dad said the pup belonged to the whole family, but I named him Howard and he was mine. I immediately began training him, walking him, feeding him, sleeping with him. Three months later while I was in school he ran out of the house to greet my dad and was run over by a car.

I was a very self-controlled kid. Besides when I was little, I can only remember two times when I sat on my bed and cried. The first was when a girl named Nancy broke up with me in junior high, even though we hadn't actually dated. This was the other.

After a few years, I began asking for another dog. Two weeks after I left the house for college, dad brought a dog home, a stray mutt he rescued from an alley garbage can. She needed a lot of care and attention. They had to clean up after her and listen to her bark on and on about random things.

That's when I realized who the household pet had been all those years.

PAPER TRAINING

Little Jack Horner sat in a corner
Eating his Christmas pie
He stuck in his thumb, pulled out a plum
And said, "What a good boy am I!"

After reading that, I headed for the kitchen, my size 3 Keds squeaking across the linoleum. I stuck my thumb directly into Mom's freshly baked pie. As I pulled out my thumb, the golden, steaming crust broke open like a volcano. It was an apple pie, as it turned out. The sticky, boiling hot sugar syrup emptied my brain of plums. I screamed and did the hot thumb dance. Mom looked over her shoulder and, without any mention whatsoever about what a good boy was I, whacked me with a newspaper.

I love the newspaper, which is surprising considering my upbringing. I read it cover to cover every day. My parents did too, especially on Sunday. The Sunday special sections would be strewn about our big dining table like assorted chocolates, anchored with cups of hot coffee.

I never saw my parents roll a newspaper into a weapon. Perhaps there were fifty of them stashed strategically about the house, or maybe my parents kept one in a holster strapped to their thigh. When our family dog got sick and started to barf, preceded by that goose-like *honk...honk...honk...*, Dad yelled "No!" and swatted her on the flank with a newspaper produced from thin air, as if it had been resting like a loaded mousetrap under his trigger finger.

OF MICE AND ME

When I feel like I might throw up, I need someone to pet my back and softly repeat, "Oh, poor baby. Oh, poor baby." To be swatted mid-barf with a newspaper would be an awful indignity.

I got a puppy and a little sister at about the same time, although I think it was a coincidence. When the time came for potty training, the puppy got the newspaper like a Steve Gadd drum solo, but my sister Jodi didn't get swatted once. Maybe, like me, she learned by watching. Dad always said I could learn a lot from a newspaper. I think that's why they say it smarts.

Newspapers don't really hurt that much, but the noise makes such a startling crack that you think it *should* have hurt, so you cry just in case.

Smarting on my behind and in my heart, betrayed by my *Little Golden Book of Nursery Rhymes* which had been planted on me by my very own mother, who was now putting her smoking newspaper back into its holster, I protested.

"I only did it because Jack did it first!"

Whack! again.

I forgot: Jack is my Dad's name too.

MOUSE POOP

We were hiking a remote trail in Iowa's Loess Hills when we discovered something curious: little white droppings about the size of dog poop dotting the trail every twenty feet or so. I picked one up.

Light as cotton candy, it appeared to be made of compressed fur, nearly white. I gingerly picked up a second one. A third had tiny little feet in it.

Owl pellets, I guessed. But why only on the trail? Owls don't hike.

All my sisters are geniuses. One is a nerdist in all things outdoors, so I asked her: Are there other animals that poop furry thumb-sized rodents? And why was the hair almost always ash-white?

Her response:

Okey dokey, hmmm… let's examine the facts.

Owls tend to ralph over the edge of the branch they are sitting on, and pellets come from the uppy end of the owl and not the downy end. They are lovely, dry papery cocoons of fur and bone about the length of a thumb. Baby owls have smaller, marshmallow-size pellets with whatever fragments of creature the mom owl rammed down their throat.

OF MICE AND ME

As they get older, you can see the bones evolve from little mousy heads and toes to broken squirrel femurs and the partial skulls of very small children with buck teeth. Well, maybe they're rabbit skulls, but we don't seem to have as many kids in the neighborhood as we used to.

So what scatalagous treasure do YOU have? Since the evidence was on a trail, I'm guessing fox or coyote. They have territories with trails they follow habitually and while they're looking up into the trees trying to avoid owl vomit, some poop falls out their nether end. Around here, the coyote scat has a lot of either deer hair from scavenging carcasses or snowshoe hare hair, so they seem white. Older poop also appears white from the calcium, I'm guessing, not quite digested from the bones. I suppose it could also be powdered sugar, I'm not a wildlife expert.

The little bones are certainly fascinating. Last night I came across a partially dissolved owl pellet from the family of horned owls we had here last year and there was a perfect little mouse skull with all its microscopic teeth intact, packed gently in the dry fluff of intestinally compressed rabbit down. I have a bowl of owl pellets in my glass bookcase. Saving them for a special occasion, I suppose.

Are you enjoying the freedom of life after bar? I want you to be happy dearie, you're my favorite, after all.

Hmmm. I didn't pick at the poop too much, because I don't remember the last time I had a tetanus shot. Although we found a few bone bits, tiny and probably broken, I imagine they had been chewed, so the fox theory makes sense. The hair could have been deer, or any of the rodents that hide in those ominous cliffside holes.

Owls don't really chew. It's no fault of their own that they don't have teeth (thank Heaven) so I would expect more complete skeletons, tails, toenails, and shirt buttons. Now that I have more information, I intend to go back and pick at more poop.

During a morel-hunting hike I came home with: 1 complete rabbit skull, it's bones fragile and tissue-thin; 5 ticks; and 0 morels. I bleached the wee skull and set it outside to bask in the sun until it was pearl white. I hung it on my kitchen wall, a talisman to make me king of the rabbits.

My girlfriend's big yard has no coyotes, owls, nor cats, so she has mice instead. She tried to be tolerant and generous, but due to lots of springtime mousie-panky, their numbers grew into an intolerably large and opportunistic community. It seems all forms of traps and poisons are stomach-churning — worse for the mice even — so I wrote my sister again for advice.

She replied:

> *I LOVE mousies. However, when they start filling your oven with dog food copped out of the doggie dish in the dark of the night, it's time for disciplinary action.*
>
> *Sticky traps are perverted versions of the La Brea tar pits but for mice. Horrible and traumatizing (at least to me).*

OF MICE AND ME

I found some interesting little live traps that work on the principles of greed and balance. Mousie goes in and when he reaches that little blob of peanut caviar in the back, the assembly tilts and the door flops shut. Works pretty darned good. Open the door and the mousie shoots out like a bottle rocket. Startling the first time, especially if you point it at your face. Wear safety glasses.

However, I ended up laying awake at night waiting for that "click," not wanting the little critter to linger in that claustrophobic environment for even a few minutes. I once had a mousie trapped all night and when I dumped him out, he was soaking wet from the moisture escaping both ends. Also, if your mice are chubby from all the dog food, they may not fit. I had dainty little deer mice; I'm not sure some of those mongo Omaha honkers could even get their heads in.

Spring traps have to be set right at the edge of walls or cabinets, not in the middle of the room where you might catch a cat. Cats will sue your ass.

Peanut butter is the absolute best catching food, bar none. It's so sticky that by the time they've licked their chops and swallowed it, they're so exhausted they stagger into the tripping mechanism. Watch out for the Salmonella peanut butter, it might kill them.

Once you catch a mouse, empty its pockets. They carry maps. Doesn't matter how many times I've dumped one of those little dudes outside, they find their way back to my silverware drawer by the next day.

You can't beat 'em, you can't join 'em, you can't kill 'em. It's all just too sentimental. It's too bad I don't feel the same way about humans.

WHEELS

HECK ON WHEELS

My first tricycle was twice as tall as everyone else's. My feet barely reached the pedals. It was a hand-me-down, apparently owned by someone who rode it at age fifteen.

Kids were less judgmental then. We rode what we were given and made it work. I was given that tricycle, and I didn't think about anything except how to grow into it.

Because its front wheel was so much bigger then other trikes, mine was way faster. Due to its height, it cornered like a fifteen-high stack of hay bales, again and again planting me face first into the corner lot's scratchy zoysia.

My little friend Eric and I were curious and handy. Soon we discovered we could disassemble our trikes into a pile of curved pipes and greasy bearings. Goofing around one day, we discovered we could reassemble a trike upside down: put the front wheel where the handlebars had been, and vice-versa. Flip the whole thing over, put the seat between the back wheels and — *jeepers!* We had invented the Big Wheel! Only we called it a chopper, because it looked sort of like one and the Big Wheel hadn't been invented yet.

When the *other* Big Wheel made its debut, I felt we were being spied upon. The Big Wheel was smaller than my trike and made of Barbie-colored plastic, but otherwise looked suspiciously similar. I had grown a bit by the time it debuted, so tall that my knees banged into the handlebars and the back axle sagged under my weight, bowing the fat tires inward—but I gamely gave it a try. It made a weird, rattly drum sound as I pedaled, like the empty plastic tub it was.

One day my dad offered to take me to Western Auto Hardware to buy a bicycle. It was another random act, in keeping with his parenting style, entirely independent of any begging I had done here or there. But when you are one among six kids and Dad is in a giving mood, you take.

I picked out a honey-gold Schwinn Sting-Ray with a long banana seat and high handlebars we called "ape-hangers." The back tire was a fat, treadless drag-racing thing they called a "slick."

It was a two-speed: crazy cool technology that shifted gears when you kicked the pedals lightly backwards, giving the pause-and-go feel of a real car. Kicking backwards also engaged that fat back tire brake, so I had to master the hairline difference between the shift and the somersault.

It was new. It was mine. Not a hand-me-down, but *my own new bike*. It was gold. It was beautiful. In two weeks, it was stolen.

My father railed and spit at how careless I had been to park it in front of our house, where I had parked every riding toy I had ever owned since birth. For years it had been my parking lot. Today: how could I be so stupid?

After lots of stomping and spitting and ranting that I'd never own another thing as long as I lived if I didn't take care of it, he took me back to Western Auto. I picked out a gleaming purple Sting-Ray, a single-speed this time, in humble penance because I didn't feel I deserved another two-speed.

After a spate of thefts not limited to our front yard, Dad built a metal shed with a locking door. He bought us each a bike lock too, as insurance. Soon thereafter, my brother's three-speed Schwinn English Racer was stolen, and we all twittered about who might have broken into our tin Fort Knox. The bike lock was melted through. *Melted!* Surely it was my older brother's creepy friends, we murmured, hands a-wringing. I loved the drama, when it wasn't about me.

Weeks passed. Our fair city's flock of Sherlocks turned up nothing. His bike was gone for good.

Then it came as if out of nowhere: The Orange Krate. It fell out of Heaven for my brother.

The Orange Krate was a revolutionary bicycle of the 1970s: dual hand-brakes, front and rear shock absorbers, and five speeds controlled by a "Stik Shift." Not a little flick-lever — a real six-inch-long shift handle with an engraved ball on the end, suitable for a Camaro. The front tire was half as big as the rear, clearly to take advantage of the aerodynamic forces one could achieve exploiting this technology. It sported a drum brake — no mortal bicycle brake would stop this hot witch. It even had a flared rear fender to keep the bike under control at supersonic speeds.

Having a drum brake, shock absorbers and gearshift in the '70s is the equivalent of having X-ray vision and nuclear missiles on your bike today. Without them, you are a mere minion.

The bike came with other color-coded names: Apple Krate, Cotton Picker, Grey Ghost, Lemon Peeler, and Pea Picker. What kid wanted a bike the color of peas?

My brother's friends gathered in admiration. Wide-eyed, I touched the shift lever. Instantly I was pummeled with a screaming chorus of 15-year-old car-alarm voices: "Don't touch that! You'll strip the gears! You'll strip the gears! *You'll strip the gears!*" I never touched it again, but I began to wish someone would steal it.

"How could you be so stupid?"

That again. Older people say it as if little boys were born forty years old, as if they might have *tried* to be stupid. "Well, since you asked, here's the trick I figured out to being so stupid..."

But I wasn't stupid. Not even then, I knew it. Eric and I know we invented the Big Wheel—er, *chopper.*

So then, who *did* invent the Big Wheel proper? Mattel? Kenner? Fisher Price? Hasbro? Nope: Louis Marx and Company. *Who?* They were a big deal in 1920, no so much in 1950, except for that Big Wheel thing, and not at all in 1972, when they were bought by Quaker Oats. Even their logo was forgettable: a big MAR with a vague X through the middle, kind of like a railroad crossing sign. The X usually went unnoticed, so people called them Mar toys.

The Louis Marx slogan was:

> "One of the many Marx toys, have you all of them?"

Forgettable, maybe, but their grammar was tops.

CRUNCH TIME

When I was in high school I bought an MGA, a sweet two-seat sports car made in Great Britain. It was only $500, because its owner had driven it into a pole so hard its headlights met up on the other side. The damage cost me $1000 to fix, so at $1500 it was still a pretty good deal. I sold it three years later to buy a wedding ring.

The first car crash I was invited to was when I was riding my motorcycle and three high school classmates ran a red light. I T-boned them. I was speeding as always, which might have been helpful this time because I jumped right before the impact and flew over the whole unfortunate mess. Time slowed down, so I had plenty of opportunity to view my pie-eyed friends through the windshield as I sailed by. That crash cost me $600, because they lied to their dads about the red light. I didn't get screwed again until, as I said, I sold that MG.

Five years later I was changing lanes in my Chevy panel van when a guy tried to pass me. Everyone passed my van, so I should have expected it. I dinged his fender. His fender dinged me for $300.

Although plenty of people have taken little potshots at my cars since then, I was never around so I never knew who to shoot. Twenty-five years passed without me being in a major accident, which is surprising given how I drive. I once went from downtown to my midtown house at 70 MPH. I hit all the green lights — maybe because they were set for 35 MPH.

Like everything else over the years, crashes have changed. As the saying goes, they don't make 'em like they used to.

I borrowed my wife's shiny new silver truck to pick up a few groceries, and as I was leaving I accidentally backed into a light pole that was wisely planted in a barrel-shaped concrete base. I was going 1 MPH, which is slow even for going backwards. It is a high-tech vehicle, with airbags in the front for head-ons and airbags on the sides for T-bones. It doesn't have an airbag on the back for light poles.

I heard an unsettling little crunch, so I figured I cracked the plastic cover over the spare tire. Although it costs them $3 to manufacture one, I knew it would cost me $250 to replace it. I didn't even bother to look until I got home. I didn't worry about the bumper, because bumpers are designed to bump. When I finally took a look, it appeared that the pole my MG once hit had exacted its revenge. Her truck may have been made in Japan, but the bumper was made of china.

I didn't know where to take it for repair, because thankfully I don't know anybody in the business. I asked a friend, "You've had body work done, right? Who did you use?" She looked down at her sweater and back at me, mouth agape. "No," I added quickly, "your son's car — remember?" So I guess I got two answers.

Body shops all charge pretty much the same these days. They type what damage is done and how well you're dressed into a computer, and it prints a bill. Body shops used to be gritty affairs, but the one I went to had a waiting room clean as a dentist's office, with the same magazines and the same drill noises.

A bumper only has one job to do. It is supposed to let you bump things. These days bumpers are ugly but resilient, with pistons and springs and flexi-bendy stuff, and a plastic cover to make it all presentable. I had hoped to replace only the crinkled facade, which I figured these days would cost $1000. Ironically, that part was only $250. I saw it there in the middle of the estimate, which was $3,118.

They smiled and waved as I left, knowing they had made another boat payment. As I left the parking lot I drove forward, right over the curb, because I couldn't afford to back up again.

DRIVING LESSONS

When my twin daughters neared sixteen years old I forced driving upon them. I love to drive, and learned when I was thirteen. It baffled me how many of their friends were seventeen or eighteen before bothering to take their driver's test. Are their parents that fun to drive around with? To me, driving was up there with the Statue of Liberty and the right to vote. If you're an American, it's what you do. It's your declaration of independence.

Technically, I first drove at the age of two, when I kicked the family station wagon into neutral while playing "car" and rolled down a hill into traffic. I steered, in as much as I wiggled the steering wheel back and forth, but my little legs couldn't possibly reach the brakes. But I was thirteen before I actually swiped a set of car keys and *drove*.

I was so eager to drive that I didn't see the dark intentions of Mr. Mxxxx when he offered to let me drive his long, floppy Impala. The kind, lanky man who lived around the corner encouraged me to sit on his lap and take the wheel. Soon I had his Chevy bouncing like a motorboat over country gravel at sixty miles per hour, a spiral of dust in my wake.

He had other lessons he wanted to teach me out there in the middle of nowhere. I didn't ever feel in danger. He accepted *no*. I didn't even condemn him for his advances. I just wanted to drive his car.

OF MICE AND ME

I remember vividly the feel and smell of driving fast, but it was many years before the rest of my memories of Mr. Mxxxx[24] slithered out of the dark.

At fourteen, I got a job clearing tables at a fancy restaurant, fancy as a restaurant got in our town, fancy enough that you'd wear your good boots and take off your hat. A sweet waitress named Rachel sometimes gave me a ride home. She drove a long, silver Cutlass. The horn was a chrome bar curved inside the steering wheel like a big honking smile. The manual shift lever was attached to the steering column like an oversized turn signal, skinny as my arms. The silver grill was as wide and crooked as my grin.

I'd beg her to let me drive, and eventually the five-minute lift grew into a half-hour adventure, bouncing and swaying over loose gravel backroads.

We'd often stop to talk, maybe near one of the sand pit lakes, a parking lot, or atop a country hill. At some point I slid across the squeaky vinyl bench seat and we tried to kiss. No talk, no schmoozing — we just started. Neither of us knew how, and neither admitted it. We puckered up tight, like you'd kiss your grandma, and inched closer. Her eyes were shut. Mine were wide open.

Just as I was getting used to the idea of touching someone else's mouth, she stuck out her tongue a little, like a worm from an apple. I nearly jumped out the window. I expected her to laugh at me, but her eyes were as nervous and disoriented as mine. I could see she did it because she thought she was supposed to. That's how I felt too. I dared to brush my fingers lightly across her breast through the deep, scratchy weave of her polyester waitress uniform. That was all we could handle and she drove me home. We never spoke of it again.

---

24 I'm not protecting his identity. He's dead. I'm protecting his daughter, someone I like, who doesn't know this story.

When my dad began teaching me to drive at fifteen, he thought I was a prodigious student, and I let him believe it because that felt better than having him know I was a sneak. He probably knew anyway, and was just proud of me for being able to keep a secret. Regardless, fifteen minutes after I turned sixteen I had my driver's license. I never saw Rachel again.

Prom was coming up and my dad's frumpy Datsun B210 sedan wouldn't do, so my friend Odee loaned me his gleaming, forest green Dodge Scamp. We buffed it to a spotless gloss, a boy's way of primping for a date. Odee sprayed the front seat with Armor-All to make it slick, his trick to make my date slide into me every time I turned right. What was I supposed to do with that? I couldn't drive in circles all the way to the prom, and I was certain she wouldn't appreciate getting all dressed up just to go on an arcade ride.

Odee had as much experience at romance as I did. My date managed to stay in her seat just fine, although we did park in a secluded spot and talk a while after the dance. Twenty minutes later Odee's 500-watt stereo whimpered to silence, having drained the battery dead, and we had to hike down the highway to bum a ride, she in her frilly white prom dress, I in my mint green tuxedo.

My dad once made me drive off a highway onto the gravel shoulder at 60 miles per hour so I would know how it feels if it happened in real life. I'm grateful he didn't think I needed practice driving off a cliff. I passed that lesson on, in my own way. My girls know how it feels to skid sideways on the ice in a top-heavy SUV. And when I bought them their first car, I made sure they knew how to use the jumper cables I put in the trunk.

BADASS

I like riding my bike. I like the stuff that goes with it: anybody looks tougher in black biking pants, black leather mesh gloves, black sunglasses. My bike is silver, because I wasn't thinking ahead.

I grew up riding a Sting-Ray. It had one speed. Riding it was easy. You got on, and you went. Nobody wore helmets then, as you can tell from talking to people of my generation. We didn't wear gloves or bike pants or even sunglasses. When I see little kids wearing bike helmets today, I say, "Good for you!" while I secretly whisper, "…you little sissy."

Going for a proper ride requires preparation:

1. *Pump up the tires*
2. *Put on my helmet*
3. *[crunch]*
4. *Take off my helmet*
5. *Take sunglasses out of helmet*
6. *Strap helmet on again*
7. *Put my sunglasses on*
8. *Take my helmet back off*
9. *Find the missing lens*
10. *Helmet on, sunglasses on*

11. *Attach keys to bike bag — bike pants don't have pockets*
12. *Carry my bike up from the basement*
13. *Balance it precariously on the steps while I unhook the keys from the bag to unlock the door*
14. *Clip keys back into bike bag*
15. *Saddle up and lock my feet in the pedal clips*
16. *Take feet back out; forgot my water bottle!*
17. *Door's locked, go back to bike, get door keys*
18. *Get water bottle*
19. *Stop to use the bathroom again, just to be safe*
20. *Stop by the mirror and flex*

This can go on for a while.

I planned an epic ride because I was free all day. I didn't really feel like riding, but after seeing pictures of myself from a recent event I figured I needed the exercise more than I needed what I really wanted: a margarita. Dutifully I went through the above steps, but with one addition: it was late on an overcast day, yet I wanted to wear sunglasses anyway because that's when the bugs come out. I have biking glasses with interchangeable lenses. One set is amber to improve contrast and visibility, perfect for just such an hour. I popped out the existing lenses with my thumb, then discovered these weren't my biking glasses.

Finally I was on my way. I hit the street, turned the corner, and rolled down the long, long hill we call The Grinder. As I approached warp speed I hit a swarm[25] of gnats. They pelted my sunglasses, stung my shirt, filled my nose. I couldn't take in a good breath, and dared not open my mouth to scream. I looked like I had been assaulted by a pepper mill.

---

25 Flock?

Bike pants are made of stretchy Lycra, with extra elastic in the waist and around both thighs. Very flattering. There's also a little cushy pillow sewn into the butt that is flattering only to baboons. The elastic waistband in my bike pants chose this moment to surrender. A lot has been asked of it lately. When the waist elastic fails, the rest of the stretchy material is free to pull down.

The little cushion pad now looked less like a baboon butt and more like a full diaper. Instead of protecting my bum when I sat, it was now bunched up under my nether bits, about as comfortable as sitting on a softball.

I no longer felt badass. Usually I glare encroaching cars into submission, but more of them than usual were rolling through stop signs at me. Instead of giving me plenty of clearance, more pokey pedestrians were ambling in front of me, forcing me to weave around them. I felt like I was at Wal-Mart.

Epic Ride was downgraded to Quick Spin. I putted around the neighborhood until I had fulfilled the distance rule, which is to ride for more time than I had spent getting ready. As I took the last turn toward my house, I passed a pretty young pedestrian who lowered her eyes the way a person does when encountering someone intimidating. *I still got it,* I thought.

When I spied my reflection in a window, I saw what I still had: two thousand squashed bug eyeballs ogling back at me.

Got home. Dismounted. Took a quick drink from the water bottle. No kickstand, found a place to lean the bike. Helmet off, sunglasses back in helmet. Peel gloves off.

[pause]

Wait.

[fumble, fumble]

Where are my keys?

A BANG-UP JOB

They call it the Peanut.

This peanut is 230 feet wide and 90 feet across. By my calculations it would make 37,000 jars of peanut butter, except that everybody has driven all over it and it is made of concrete.

Technically, the Peanut is a "roundabout." It isn't round. It sits at the intersection of North 50th Street and Seward. And Country Club Avenue. And North Saddle Creek Road. And Happy Hollow Boulevard. Joining eight weaving, intersecting streets, it is an octopus throwing up his arms in confusion. With the addition of little triangular traffic islands, there are a total of fifteen ways in and out of the Peanut. It was designed to simplify the intersection.

The Peanut was initially covered in cinderblock, which they later replaced with grass in a beautification project. Because so few people can navigate its zig-zaggy bends, the grass has mostly been run over.

One day I entered the Peanut right behind a big white utility van. The van stopped unexpectedly in front of me, halfway into the intersection. I had barely begun my turn when I saw his backup lights come on.

He wouldn't. He *wouldn't*.

He did. The two horn buttons on my Honda Accord were each about the size of a quarter. Banging on the center of the steering wheel doesn't do anything but deploy the airbag. The horn buttons are hard to find when you're driving straight and have plenty of time. When you're on the Peanut, honking is a game of Whac-A-Mole.

My horn never did make a noise. His big truck had a backup beeper, but it barely got one beep out before he crushed my passenger door. Mr. Van then began to drive off. I took chase. My first thought: "Your fat-ass van got nuthin' on my Honda." I was almost disappointed when he decided to pull over in a nearby parking lot. We got out and shared our opinions of each other's driving.

He accused me of following too closely, which on any given day might have been true, but I reminded him in this case he was backing up, and I was stationary. I was *sideways*. When another driver pulled up and said he saw the whole thing, Whitey Van Man got nicer. He didn't have anything to write with or on. I'm a writer, so I always have a pen. I took out a business card and watched him write down his name and phone number. I asked for his insurance information, and he wrote that on another card. I then handed him a business card to keep and, after promising to take care of things, he drove off.

When I got home I realized the card I had given him was the card with his insurance info on it. I think he realized it too. So now I had only his first name and a cell number, which of course he stopped answering. After much searching but no finding, and months of shrugs from the police, I gave up.[26]

The other culprit we don't know is Who Designed the Peanut. I have orated on the need for a big plaque in his honor so we can refer to it by its more proper name, like The Bilbo Bongwater Roundabout Debacle, or The Horatio Huey Hootenanny — Huey Hooey for short. Instead of cursing it generically, I'd like to get specific.

---

26 His name is Mike Muhleka. If you know him, tell him he owes me $3500.

A few days later, after no response from Boobus Van Hittenrun, I staked out the Peanut to see if he might drive by again. There I sat, wearing dark glasses and everything, scrutinizing every car. People avoid you when you sit in your car in an empty parking lot and stare. It's fun. What wasn't fun was discovering that one out of five vehicles is a white van.

Another observation I made: while navigating the serpentine legume, one in three cars bounced over a curb, and one hundred percent of those had drivers who were on the phone, each one exclaiming *"Shit!"* as they interrupted their blather about what's for dinner.

The Peanut would be a good metaphor for life, except life doesn't have someone to blame for it.

CLUTCH MOMENT

"Is a stick-shift hard to learn?"

"Nearly impossible."

"Then why do we have to learn it?"

"Because someday you may find yourself in an emergency." My daughters could always sense when I was winging it. "Maybe the only car available to go get help will be a stick-shift."

They returned blank looks while I thought some more. "All the best sports cars are stick-shift."

Without another word, they both leapt into my 1988 stick-shift Celica convertible. Learning to drive in a convertible is humbling: everyone can see your wild eyes, laugh at your jerking head and hear your pleas to God.

I picked out a good, safe spot. A former horse-racing track in my neighborhood had been turned into a giant, vacant parking lot with plenty of room for lurching and careening. Occasionally I'd encounter another parent teaching his kid to drive, and we'd stay well clear of each other in this giant game of pinball.

"Ease the clutch out slo — "

Bam! The car leapt into the air, than landed with a bounce, the engine silent.

" — wly."

What would we wear out first: the clutch or the starter?

I'd done this before, so I had some experience. I'd already made an appointment with my chiropractor.

"Give it a little more gas," I told Kate. "Then gen — "

My voice was drowned out by the whining engine spinning up to nuclear reactor velocity.

"Don't — "

Screeeee! The front tires smoked and squawked. Our skulls crushed into the headrest and the skin on our faces pulled back on our heads. She panicked, instinctively yanking her foot off the gas and stomping the brake. *Whap!* We launched face first into the dashboard, then bounced upright like three wide-eyed bobble-head dolls, as silent as the stalled engine.

Kate continued to look straight ahead as she asked, "Is it Molly's turn yet?"

I'm not stupid. I didn't start them on a stick-shift. I used an old truck, an automatic, white with rust accents, to teach them the basics: how steering feels, how to brake gently, where the ignition and turn signals are. But that's not *driving*.

One day after a hard snow I took them out to practice skidding precariously, under the presumption that I was showing them how easily the truck will twirl out of control, and how to correct it. Secretly I just wanted to spin my truck around on the ice. I hit the gas and threw it into a tight turn. They shrieked and I grinned as the back end lost traction, passed the front end, and we were sliding sideways. The tires hit a dry patch, gripped, and the truck lurched onto the two passenger-side wheels, where it teetered precariously for a moment while we all said silent prayers to the Holy Giver of Gravity. She blessed us by dropping the truck down upright.

"That completes our skid lesson," I said in a voice with a slight yodel. "You get the idea. Who wants hot chocolate?"

They both answered in unison, which sounds weird when it comes from twins. I suppose at some point they have since learned to drive in the snow.

The idea of real-world practice seemed sound. I had an inspiration: parking practice! Soon we were back at our vacant lot, which still had its faded yellow parking stripes.

"Okay, here's the deal," I explained. "I'm going to choose a parking stall and stand in front of it. You have to park in that spot without ever crossing any of the yellow lines."

With foresight I had chosen to regress to our white truck for this exercise. Parking would require brain cells which were currently being devoted entirely to the clutch, and it is an indignity to be run over by one's own car.

This will be fun! Nobody ever gave me parking stall lessons. I was proud of myself as I got out and walked about fifty feet away. I planted my feet, arms authoritatively on my hips, pointed at the spot and nodded a go-ahead.

The truck sat still for a long time. A very long time. Maybe they didn't understand the directions? I nodded again. Point-point-point. I couldn't make out their faces through the reflection of the windshield. Were they nervous? Comparing notes? It occurred to me this was the first time they were in charge of a vehicle without me in it.

Finally, the truck began to move, slowly, gently, deliberately down the aisle, carefully between the yellow guides. It passed the end of the lane, drove across the parking lot, around behind the old abandoned stadium and left the parking lot.

"Heh, that was a good one," I chuckled after an awkward few minutes. "They'll be back any minute."

Heh. Any minute.

Molly is an irreverent little cuss. Once in a restaurant she jokingly loaded a straw full of Coke and aimed it right at me, just an inch from my nose. I didn't even blink. "Go ahead," I said flatly, channeling my best Clint Eastwood. The brain can calculate a thousand possible consequences in a second. I saw all one thousand pass behind her eyes, then all I saw was Coke.

The look on her face as I regained my vision was a combination of "That was awesome" and "I'm dead." I saw that same expression on her face as the truck finally crept back into view after a long ten minutes had passed. "Sorry, you get an F on that exercise," I said. "You drove over the line."

Eventually they learned the musts of driving basics: how to cruise carefully down residential streets, creep quietly into the garage, stay off the crosswalk, hang a fast-food tray on the window, and reset the radio buttons. With a scream worthy of Robert the Bruce they entered busy Leavenworth Street, which has four lanes so narrow even experienced drivers cheat two wheels into the wrong lane. "DAD!" they cried out at every oncoming car, as if I too wasn't facing death head-on. Step by step by terrifying step, they learned to drive.

Because I cherished my little red convertible, I bought them their own car, a perky little red Acura with a snappy engine and a sexy stick-shift. Soon they were flipping gears up and down as if the shift lever was a third arm.

I expected accidents. Molly, in particular, inherited her father's lead foot. Forget the car — I prayed only that their precious, lanky, sun-goldened bodies would be spared. But not one scratch on any of our three cars could be attributed to them, except maybe the multiple door dings from one car door hitting the other car in the garage. Apparently they can't remember we own two cars.

They grew up and moved to colleges where cars were impractical. The sexy little red Acura sat lonely and unused. It hurt to sell it, like selling an era.

Last summer the old truck, now rust-colored with white accents, lost its transmission. The following autumn my convertible caught fire and burned to the ground.[27]

As far as I know they have never had a car crash. Last week, borrowing my wife's brand new truck, I backed into a light pole in an empty parking lot while driving at 1 mph and caused $3000 damage to the "flexible" bumper. So kids, let that be a lesson to you.

---

27 That's another story. See the upcoming chapter, "My Hot Car."

MY HOT CAR

Just two years before, the Spotted Tail Wildfire charred 17,000 acres of pristine prairie around Chadron, Nebraska. Firefighters fought it for a week. You'd think there wouldn't be anything left to burn, but you'd be surprised: prairies are remarkably resilient and sometimes even benefit from such a calamity.

I thought of that as my Toyota Celica, ablaze, rolled off the highway into the tall, golden autumn grass. Things were about to go from bad to worse. Lots worse. I imagined my deer-eyed headshot in the *Alliance Times-Herald* above the caption, "Newly Recovered Prairie Torched by Omaha Idiot. Again."

But the grass, tall as the door handle, didn't ignite. Not much, anyway—just a little oval scorch beneath the car. Not for lack of trying: flames were shooting out of my car, blue and fast as a jet, then billowed high, black, and red as if it had been sponsored by British Petroleum.

Bystanders said the grass survived thanks to some rain the night before. I knew better. God himself was standing next to me, pinching his nose, shaking his head, bailing me out one more time.

Was it bad luck that my beloved convertible, my loyal playmate for twenty years, caught fire in the middle of nowhere? Or was it *good* luck that we had plenty of time to get out safely and rescue most of our gear? The conflagration didn't get going until at least five minutes after blue smoke first burst out of the dashboard vents, filling the cab as we were sailing seventy miles per hour over the winding highway, and the brake pedal flopped flaccidly to the floor. The emergency brake lasted long enough for us to slow the car onto the shoulder and pull a Fred Flintstone with our feet to finish the stop. We had plenty of time to grab our bags and my beloved guitar before the emergency brake melted and the car crept slowly down the road, silent but for the soft crunch of gravel under its tires. It wandered over the shoulder, into the ditch and onto the open prairie as if looking for a perfect picnic spot. I always thought of "blazing speed" as being faster than a stroll in the grass, but there you go. We had plenty of time before the seats and the cloth top ignited, before the gas tank melted and fierce flames leapt in triumph.

There was one bag that didn't make it, a little bathroom bag, the last one in the trunk. I thought Laura got it, she thought I did. Not much in it besides toothpaste, shampoo, and the brand-new $800 red titanium-framed eyeglasses that I had insisted she buy. I headed toward the car to get it. Laura's "NO!" was nearly drowned out by the first exploding tire, followed eventually by three more impressive blasts. I stayed put.

The lone volunteer fireman, who arrived just in time to admire the fading embers, pointed with amusement at the good-as-new, still shiny right-rear fender, its tire untouched because it was upwind of the conflagration.

"But I distinctly heard four tires blow," I said. He pointed into the gaping trunk at the spare, curled open like a spring daisy.

"Anyone bring marshmallows?" he chuckled. *Asshole*, I thought, before it occurred to me that I did. This had been a camping trip, and we had some marshmallows left in a plastic tub sitting on the side of the highway.

I took one last look at the car, incinerated to ash but for a few napkin-sized sheets of melted windshield draped like a peeling sunburn over the silver-black skeleton that had been my dashboard, its bald-wire nervous system dangling below. Balanced delicately on the frame was that pair of titanium glasses, now silver and empty of lenses.

I bought that guitar in 1988, nearly the same time as the Celica. I spent all of the tax return I had received as a reward for being recently divorced and unemployed. Both car and guitar are symbols of my phoenix past. Maybe the car took the symbolism too far.

I keep vehicles a long time. This summer I parted with my truck of 15 years. Erratic electronics and rusted suspension had withered it like Alzheimer's. How do you pick the day to give in? I had pondered the same with my beloved Celica, still sporty and tart thanks to the truck sacrificing itself for the winter driving. The Red Sled had become my only vehicle, and I knew its day would come soon. But as I stood on the high hill in the stiff breeze, after a long, perfect fall weekend cruising through the mountains and before her first bitter slog through an Omaha winter, I thought, "So *that's* how she's gonna go out."

They say death comes in threes, which has been true for me if I can count people and cars together, which I can, because I love both about equally.

Two perfectly good friends keeled over unexpectedly, plus the car thing. All three were having great fun surrounded by pals when struck down, the only real difference being that my two human friends just stopped functioning and did not spontaneously combust, which was best for all involved.

I had been with my car for exactly twenty years. With help from friends, I eked out the next few weeks with borrowed wheels while I sorted out a new relationship. Every time I went to my garage it startled me to see a big white Chevy pickup where my little red Toyota used to be. With people, we mourn alone for a while before replacing them. With cars, you have to move along.

I knew my little Celica her whole life — she was the first car I ever bought new — and I was accustomed to her quirks and habits. She was in lovely shape after all these years, a pleasure to look at, nimble and efficient — the Japanese age very well. Her temporary replacement is classically Midwestern: white, sturdy and reliable. Where my old girl was the type you'd invite on an autumn picnic in the country, the temp is who you'd call if you needed to move a dresser.

Through a mutual friend, I met a Honda Accord. She's older too, has some dings under the surface and limps to the left a bit from an accident years ago, but she's real good on the inside. Besides, I ain't no spring chicken either. And as I said, in such matters one is forced to move on.

GOING DOWN

My Google home page used to present two helpful Tips of the Day. They were random. One day's tips:

1. *How to Land an Airplane in an Emergency*
2. *How to Make an Origami Picture Frame*

I shouldn't try to find create a relationship between the two, but it's my nature to connect everything into One Big Whole.

I always wanted to learn to fly an airplane, but I'm a procrastinator and still haven't finished the application form I got thirty years ago. So if I find myself at the controls of an airplane, it is already an emergency.

As for origami, I can fold a dollar into a tiny pirate hat.

I think the first thing one should do if 1) one is at the controls of an airplane; 2) one doesn't know how to fly; and 3) the plane is pointing down; one should first 4) put down the origami.

But instead, the instructions suggested, *"Take a breather."* I presume they meant to say, "Take a deep breath," because when your plane is nose down it's not a good time for a coffee break. The instructions said you might be *"overwhelmed by the gravity of the situation."* If I can count on anything in a plane crash, it's being overwhelmed by gravity.

They could have skipped the next step too: *"Keep the aircraft level."* I think in a plane emergency, that is understood to be the problem.

Next, I am instructed to *"correct the pitch and bank, simultaneously turning the yoke and pulling it, to align with the artificial horizon."* The one thing plane crashing and origami have in common is the baffling instructions.

"Call for help." Perfectly reasonable. I presume they mean over the radio.

"If a red light is lit, tell the controller. Below the red light, there will be a description of the light, i.e., "Generator," "Low Voltage," etc. Obviously this requires prompt attention." Obviously, it also helps if you know how to fix a generator while flying a plane.

The instructions go on to remind me that the "Push-to-Talk" button is right next to the "Autopilot" button, which, if pushed accidentally, could result in a crash, which I think I'm resulting in anyway.

"Give the controller the airplane's call sign. This will not only clearly identify you, but the controllers will be able to get basic information about the airplane that you probably won't know about." Like where the pilot went?

"Find the airspeed indicator." Spinning clockwise = bad. But alternately, *"Do not let the aircraft fly too slowly, especially near the ground."* Glad to know that, because if it were up to me, I'd fly really *really* slowly, really *really* near the ground, then step out.

"Never land with a full tank of fuel." Or a full bladder. Maybe now would be a good time to fold an origami diaper.

My favorite instruction came next:

"Land the plane."

Easy as that. They should have put that at the top. After I land the plane I'll get back to my other to-do list: 1) cure cancer.

"The controller will likely lead you to an airport, but if not, try to avoid obstacles." Is the ground an obstacle? I hear The Hudson River is s popular destination.

"Reduce power to idle by pulling the throttle all the way towards you. It is a black lever located between the pilot and co-pilot." This would be more helpful if we knew where the pilot and co-pilot were.

The instructions then explain that during the last few seconds I'll be using a variety of flaps, slats, throttle and reverse-thrust to slow the plane. Just in case, I'll make a little origami barf-bag.

The final step: *"Congratulations! You have landed an airplane."* My first thought was, "How do you know?" But of course if I were reading the last step, either 1) "Congratulations!" or; 2) I was skipping ahead in the instructions. Either way, the affirmation is nice.

In honor of my success, I'll save my origami parachute as a souvenir.

WHERE THE HEART IS

SPECIAL DELIVERY

My first marriage was a long time ago. We got pregnant 18 months after. I don't goof around.

The hospital where we were scheduled to deliver made us take a childbirth class. There were four sessions, one per week. We joined six other couples of the usual variety: some who want you to think they already know everything, some who ask relentless questions then don't listen to answers, and some, like us, who sit silently, saucer-eyed, minds spinning as if they had just been informed their father was David Crosby.

The first class was about feeding and bottles and how to hold a newborn so his head doesn't flop and break his neck. I wondered how babies survived before they invented school. I don't remember what the second class was about because the Q&A couple wouldn't shut up long enough for the teacher to get a theme going.

At the top of the third class the teacher announced, "We're going to watch a film—"

Mrs. Q&A started to ask whether it would be presented in VHS or Beta, but the teacher pressed on: "—all about Cesarean sections." That shut Q&A up, her mouth still open.

I froze too. *They're going to train me to go in after the baby?* I envisioned myself like Little Jack Horner, only instead of sticking in my thumb, it would be my whole hand. Instead of a pie, it would feel more like a lasagne. Instead of a plum, I would pull out my daughter.

In those days, once you had a C-section you had to deliver that way forevermore. I wondered why they bothered to stitch women back up, only to open them again later. Why not install a zipper? Or a little door? Women like Octo-Mom could harvest babies like eggs from a henhouse. You could decorate the door with a crafty little wreath, maybe tattoo some daisies around the entrance. You already have a little shrubbery.

They don't because so many women wouldn't leave the door shut. Most women I know want men to understand what they're really like on the inside. If they could just show us, they would.

All these thoughts raced through my head in one second, then the movie began and the dizzying swirl popped like a soap bubble. I learned that once a C-section begins, the father has no job whatsoever. He doesn't get to say, "Breeeaaathe," because a machine took over that job. He doesn't even get to coach, "Push, honey," because to push at that point will make the baby squirt out like a pumpkin seed.

There's no need to tell you more about the movie. You pretty much know what happens next if you saw *Alien*. I don't know why they made us watch it except to make regular childbirth, the equivalent of passing a football out your butt, look pleasant by comparison.

Contractions started three weeks early. I thought they might be false, so we waited a little while. They weren't. We rushed to the hospital, where we were issued a room and matching gowns, and we were told to wait.

At one point the attending nurse mumbled that she wasn't hearing the baby's heartbeat very well through the strapped-on monitor, so she picked up a little hand-held version and poked around for a better spot. Suddenly she stiffened and listened more intently, froze for a moment, then rushed out of the room without a word.

We exchanged worried glances. The attendant returned with the head nurse in tow, who put on headphones and listened for herself. She looked at the attendant in confirmation, and they both whisked away, avoiding eye contact with us. *Please not this*, I thought. *Please not us.*

We didn't have much money back then, and no insurance. We had skipped a lot of the pre-natal testing: no amniocentesis, no ultrasounds, paying as we went for what we could afford and only for what seemed crucial. Suddenly everything seemed crucial.

Long, quiet minutes passed before the attendant and head nurse returned with the doctor. He listened briefly, then announced flatly, "Congratulations. You're having twins."

Et voila. He left the room.

The teacher didn't cover this in class.

I tipped back into the wall. My wife let out an uncomfortable, high-pitched giggle. I wasn't unhappy with the news, just bewildered. I hadn't pictured any of this.

Events happened fast after that. Baby Kate burst into this world with a wide-eyed gasp, as one emerges from a deep dive. The doctor passed her over his shoulder to Team One, which whisked her away to a cold stainless-steel scale, where she was weighed and wiped clean of wax and debris.

Kate had cleared the way head-first. Molly followed more tentatively, her right hand outstretched to feel the way. She got stuck with her arm bent over her head. The doctor had to push her back in and rearrange her, causing New Mom to let out a wild-eyed yell fit for a Pittsburgh Steeler. Molly gave it another go and flopped out with comparative ease, probably thanks to Kate having done the spelunking. She was hustled off to a second scale, a heat lamp glaring above her face, and abandoned while the staff returned to Kate.

I had been sold on the idea of participating in the delivery, and imagined myself in full hospital uniform standing shoulder-to-shoulder with the doctor, crouched with my catcher's mitt at the ready. The reality was that I was given a taped-off square in which to stand, with firm instructions to stay there and say only the few canned phrases I was taught in class. "Push. Breathe."

I saw Molly, alone and squinting under the harsh floodlight. *Nuts to this*, I thought. *I'm breaking out.* Unseen, I crept the few steps to Molly and shaded her face with my giant adult hands. Her eyes opened wide and she looked at me as if to say, "Thanks Mister, whoever you are."

I didn't realize how wide and clear and soulful a baby's eyes are at birth. It's only after they squirt in an antibiotic that the eyes swell shut for a week, like a visit from Joe Frazier. I enjoyed a brief moment bathing Kate before they doctored her eyes shut too. So much magical gazing time is lost. If I knew then what I know now, I'd have looked deeper, longer. My eyes would have said, "We're gonna be fine," even though I didn't know.

There was nothing else for me to do. Labor had been long and I had been awake and terrified for nearly a day. I headed out to buy another crib, grateful for a task I understood, but it seemed woefully inadequate preparation for what was coming.

In the elevator I encountered our baby class teacher. Shell-shocked and exhausted, I could barely form sentences. I tried to apologize because, since we had just delivered twins, we wouldn't be attending her final class covering normal childbirth.

"How big were they?" she asked.

"Fifteen and sixteen pounds."

She fainted, right there in the elevator.

What are you *fainting for?* I thought. *You're the one who presents horror films for a living, and I'm the one who just touched two blood-soaked fetuses for the first time.*

No, wait, I remember now — the babies were five and six pounds. I didn't know at the time whether that was good or not. They probably covered that in the final class.

ICED, ICED, BABY

We weren't getting along. Mostly, we were just staying away from each other. I love to go for walks at night in the winter, and I was happy to go alone.

Winter sky is so clear it's almost black, with stars piercing holes in the velvet. I see patterns in the stars, but I don't see a dog or bear or lion. Really, Cassiopeia: you're not a queen clinging to your upturned throne. You're a "W." But you're still pretty.

Even as a child I noticed Orion. Orion followed me as I walked to visit my friend Harold. I'd speed up, slow down, break into a dead run, and Orion would always follow me apace. I didn't feel threatened as much as watched over.

It was that kind of night when I put on my sweat pants and coat to stroll the half-mile or so to Miller Park, Orion looking over my left shoulder. The park wasn't considered a safe place to go at night, but it was winter and I figured I looked as scary as anybody. Without the people, it was a magical place filled with giant cottonwood and birch trees surrounding a large frozen lagoon.

I shuffled out onto the blue-black ice, pushing tracks through the light dusting of snow. I paused in the middle of the pond, admiring its reflection of the sky, wallowing in the absolute silence. The world seemed to expand as I stood still for the longest time, watching my breath waft away. Finally I grew cold and turned for home.

Halfway back to shore I heard a muffled *chunk*. I played on the ice a lot as a kid and was used to the heavy noises it makes. But after the second *chunk,* then a third, I quickened my pace.

Crack! This one was much sharper, nearer the surface. I felt it through my shoes. I bolted. My feet spun on the ice.

Everything began to collapse. I was now running on separate pieces of ice that teetered underfoot, water splashing around the edges. It seemed I might yet stay up, like running on snowshoes, if I could go fast enough to stay ahead of the crumbling.

I didn't.

I went under, swallowed whole.

The air rushed out of my lungs as I plunged into the cold. With every maneuver to climb out, the ice broke beneath me. It was so cold I couldn't feel it. The dead quiet was replaced with a hissing noise, the fear, blood and adrenaline racing through my ears. The shore didn't seem too far away, but I couldn't get up on the ice enough to get there.

Moments later my flailing legs bumped the bottom. I gathered my footing and discovered the water was only four feet deep. I stood up, water only to my ribs. I felt stupid and thrilled at the same time. The bottom was sticky as taffy, gloopy suction tugging at my shoes. Slog by slog, chunk by chunk, I hammered my way out.

I got hypothermic once before, as an unprepared high-schooler atop a mountain in Colorado, and knew not to let that happen again. With a warm dry home only six blocks away, I ran for it. I was sure that running would keep me warm and I'd get there before everything froze up.

My legs had gone numb, but I could feel my muscles thickening. My feet grew heavier. I was slowing. I forged ahead, four blocks still to go. My run faded to a trudge, then into clumsy baby steps, then zombie shambling. I wasn't going to make it. Not even close.

Resigned and gasping, I bent over to catch my breath and looked at my mud-caked feet. They were buried under my water-soaked sweat pants. My legs had become so numb I didn't notice when the drawstring had come untied, freeing the wet, heavy sweat pants to slide their way down around my ankles.

Huh, I thought. *How about that.*

I pulled my sweatpants back up over my pink legs. A couple of quick, light test steps proved I could run just fine after all, and I sprinted home.

She looked up from her gallon jug of Gallo Hearty Burgundy through drooping eyelids as I burst through the front door, wild-eyed and dripping. I hollered a very abbreviated version of what happened (omitting the sweat pants part) as I sloshed by, heading straight for a hot bath. The lazy blink of her eyes spoke as if she had come right out and said it: *it would have been convenient if you had drowned.*

That same year, it was the marriage that went under.

Today the ice was perfect, a rare gift in the Midwest. Sleek, smooth, clear and blue, free of snow and bumps. Laura and I went ice skating, enjoying the whole lake to ourselves but for a few children and a couple of cranky ice-fishermen. Still, I kept close to the shore. I always keep close to the shore now. We slid effortlessly across the slick grayness.

Weeks later while walking the beach of Lake Manawa, we came upon three ice sailboats poised invitingly on the sand. I admired the sleek blades, the tight rigging and the vast stretch of flat ice beckoning them out to play in the middle of the lake. My imagination raced.

Someday, maybe. Someday.

I'M WITH THE BAND

It was a dream opportunity: one of my favorite bands asked me to join them.

Never mind that I was older, or that I wasn't their kind of a rocker. (I own some Spandex, but I only wear it when I run in the dark.) As much as rock bands strive to have good songs, they ache for a cool name and a great look. I had the kind of look fathers welcomed when their daughters brought me home.

I was raised on musicians like Paul Simon, James Taylor, Jim Croce and Carole King. It's not that I was destined to play that kind of singer-songwriter music. It's just that I was surrounded by it, much like being an American doesn't make you like hot dogs but you all know how to make one. To teach myself guitar, I brought home songbooks bought with my busboy earnings. I'd hole up in my bedroom, put my fingers where the little dots told me to, and learn entire albums.

I'm a solid guitarist with a good ear for harmonies, and this band needed both. Their bad-ass, dread-wearing, harmony-singing, hip-hopping bass player had been kicked out of the band for punching the lead singer in the face. Later that year he was charged with murdering his wife and throwing her off a bridge, so the band felt pretty good about their decision.

The problem was that they had just recorded a new album and there was only a month to go before their big release party. Two of us were brought in to take his place. It was a joy to learn the songs and I loved every one of them. On the day of the album release show, I stood on the stage feeling proud, but I knew I was not the first choice.

We played gigs here and there after that, each worse than before. The lowlight was a festival in the middle of a cornfield in July, on a stage made from a flatbed trailer. In the humid summer heat we stood waiting as the event planner realized they needed to run an extension cord hundreds of feet to the stage so we could plug in our amps.

Playing an acoustic guitar outdoors in the summer is like eating an ice cream cone: you have about two good minutes before everything melts. It sounds like it's wearing socks.

The lead guitarist, a wordless fellow so tall and skinny that when he put on his broad-brimmed cowboy hat he looked like the letter *T*, began making suggestions. "Why don't we hang out, just the two of us, and play some guitar?" He didn't mean, *Let's be buddies!* He meant, *Why don't you let me show you what I want you to play.*

Soon I found myself out of the band altogether.

Bands in the Midwest don't really fire a member. They usually just morph around him, like in the Ben Folds song:

> *Citing artistic differences*
> *The band broke up in May*
> *And in June reformed without me*
> *And they got a different name*

We stopped having rehearsals. There were no calls, no explanations, no questions. We all knew. The gigs stopped. After a few awkward months, we could see each other and act like nothing happened. Guys are great like that.

The reason so many bands pop up with a remix of members from other bands isn't because the guys are great pals and all hang out together for the love of music. It's because somebody got fired in the time-honored, passive-aggressive male tradition.

Guys break up bands like they break up with girls:

> *We need some time off.*
> *It's not you. We think you're great. We just want to go in a different direction.*
> *We can still hang out.*

Recently I was on the bill with a few other solo songwriters, including the former lead singer of the old band. I sat in with him on a few of his tunes, and like riding a bicycle the chords and harmonies came back. Older and paunchier, we played stripped-down acoustic versions on the small, stark stage. It felt great.

My songwriter friend Beth once said that a good song was one that worked just as well on an acoustic guitar as it does under a truckload of lights, amps and Spandex. Maybe that's why I was drawn to that rock band in the first place. I couldn't rock the look, but I sure felt the music. Now, if I could just fire the rest of the band…

THE ORIENTEER

I took an orienteering class in college. Orienteering is walking around with a compass, trying to get to a predetermined destination before everybody else. Someone tells you which way to go, and how far. Sort of like the army, without the free haircut.

For one of our exams we were instructed to drop a dime in the grass. Then the teacher gave us a complicated list of instructions:

1. *Go 72 yards at a heading of 290 degrees*
2. *48 yards at 46 degrees*
3. *91 yards at 198 degrees…*

…and so on. He designed the directions so that if I followed them correctly I would end up standing on my dime.

The first test was easy. I found my dime in the grass on the first try. I was elated, like discovering I had a secret superpower.

The exercises grew more complicated. I learned a trick: in order to get an *A* on the test, it helped to have a few extra dimes in my pocket.

With the invention of GPS, you just enter the location you want, and the device points the way. It requires about the same skill as filling out a crossword puzzle with the answer sheet in front of you. But at least you end up where you want to go, and you don't need to carry extra change.

Compasses are sexy. The invisible forces of magnetism are harnessed by your magic needle as it coaxes clues from the unseen.

Maps are like that too. They tell the future. They'll tell you a town is two miles over the hill and beyond the next left turn, which you can't even see. You go over the hill and around the corner and — *oh my God there it is!* It's like tarot cards that actually make sense.

I recently went on vacation in the Black Hills of South Dakota, where you can hike along endless breathtaking views. I bought a topographical map for ten dollars: that's cheaper than one visit to a palm reader, and with more lines. I brought my trusty compass, a nice orienteering one that lays over your map and reveals its secrets.

I pointed the compass at Black Elk Peak, the tallest mountain east of the Rockies, and took a reading: 45 degrees. Then Little Devil's Tower, the scariest cliff I've ever dangled over: 64 degrees. Cathedral Spires, a craggy, spiky formation that will give you religion: 72 degrees. On my map I drew light pencil lines through all three mountains using those vectors. The lines triangulated on one spot. *Me.*

Three mountains, each over 2 billion years old (that's 6,000 in Fundamentalist years), agreed that I exist. My head swirled at the thought. I marked a dot on the map. *Me.*

I looked up at Laura. She was eighteen feet away at 48 degrees, sitting in a camp chair atop a high cliff overlooking layers of blue-gray hills that faded into an imperceptible seam with the sky. She was wrapped in a cozy wool blanket, with a book in her lap and a margarita in her hand. Laura knows how to enjoy a view even without maps.

She saw me and smiled. "I love to watch you geek out like that."

"I'm on the map," I announced. "I'm *right here.*"

"I knew you would be."

"Will you marry me?"

"Yes."

IN STITCHES

I *hate* going to the doctor.

Still, I go every ten years or so, whether I need to or not.

Mostly, it's the waiting I hate. Who else has a room specifically named for waiting? "You'd like some new shoes? Fine. First go sit over there for a half-hour." Who else can be 45 minutes late for my appointment without getting punched in the face?

At last, you're invited into an examination room. But nope, the doctor is not there. You wait again. You hear him outside the door each time he passes, chuckling with the nurses. Eventually he bops in, cheerfully chatting about your maladies and Notre Dame, then you wait again while he leaves to look up what he's supposed to do about either of them. Most of your waiting is done half naked, sitting on the edge of a half bed, as if it's not vulnerable enough just being sick.

I want the most arrogant person in the room to be me. I want to make other people wait until I grace them with my appearance. I want to burst into the doctor's examining room saying, "I'm so *sorry* I'm late. The traffic was *terrible!* How about them Huskers?"

A doctor won't let you burst into any of his rooms, I suppose to prevent you from walking in on him with his thumb up your investment broker's butt. That wouldn't be good: how could I resist saying, "Find his head yet?"

OF MICE AND ME

I would do just about anything to avoid going to the doctor. Just about anything doesn't include cancer, so when I developed an ugly growth on my face, I went to a dermatologist. Anything that can look ugly against the backdrop of my face deserves respect.

With just a glance he announced, "It's cancer. Let's take it off right now." He began sharpening knives. "Don't worry," he added, "it's the good kind."

I didn't know there was a good kind of cancer. I tried to imagine my friends saying, "Hey — nice job on the cancer. Good choice." As I learned later, "good" cancer doesn't spread. It just looks ugly. The "bad" cancer carries a flag and marches through your body recruiting all your organs to rebel against you.

"Close your eyes," the nurse instructed. That's because closed eyes keep you from seeing your own blood squirt from your head like a squeezed lemon. He cut off the lump, leaving behind a teaspoon-sized crater. Then he proceeded with the Mohs technique, by which he chips out a little bit at a time, tests each tidbit, and comes back for more if he doesn't get all of the tumor. The idea is to leave as much of your face as possible, which I appreciate, but it was hard to smile politely every time they came back and knifed a little more from what had already been scooped. I'd like to send fan mail to the guy who invented Novocain.

What's left is an impressive scar by my left eye. I like how it looks. It gives the favorable impression that I've been in a fight, although the only knife fight I was ever in was over who got the last 50%-off Henckels chef knife at the Linens-n-Things bankruptcy sale.[28]

While removing the Big Ugly, Doc also clipped a tiny fleck off my back, a mole I didn't even know I had because I don't know any-

---

[28] I won.

thing about what's on my back. I guess when you have a scalpel in your hand, everything looks like a tumor. Two weeks later the biopsy revealed it was cancer too.

The bad kind.

There are only two ways to treat The Bad Kind: 1) Cut it out, or; 2) "palliative care," a nice way of saying make yourself comfortable for your last months on Earth. The week-long wait to learn whether you are scot-free or a short-timer feels like frozen time.

They don't do the Mohs technique for The Bad Kind. They bulldoze a parking lot around it. The scar I have looks like I got drunk in Juárez and someone stole my kidney.

After another week of waiting, I was told the doctor got it all.

Just to be safe, an oncologist checked me over like a mechanic buying a '57 Chevy. The only thing slower than a doctor's office is a radiologist's office. When you are considering how you might spend your last moments, no one chooses waiting in a doctor's office. There were only two other people in the Waiting Room. A chest X-ray takes 20 seconds, but I waited an hour to get it. Even the elevator felt slow.

But hey — you'd say — at least I still get to ride elevators.

One thing I learned during that waiting week was that I wouldn't change much about my life if I had only a year to live. I already cherish time with my wife. We already do our favorite things. I love my home. I steal every opportunity to drive my convertible and ride my unicycle. I hate wearing hats and I have to do it anyway, but that's about the only thing different.

It's a reminder that I don't have forever to get those new songs recorded, to get this book finished. No one can do it for me, so that's motivation. But it's odd to receive such a Big Mortal Warning, and to change so little about my life because of it.

The other thing I learned: the mechanic/oncologist spotted a mole under my right big toe. I must have had it all my life. Who knew?

Thanks to my newfound vulnerability, I get to visit the oncologist *and* the dermatologist twice a year from now on. Can anyone recommend a few good, long books?

NAKED POWER

My stairs squeak. When you walk up or down, it sounds like an army of marching ducks.

I don't notice the noise anymore. The house I grew up in had squeaky stairs too. I suppose it kept me from sneaking out at night, though I never had anywhere to go.

A few summers ago I was awakened with a start in the middle of the night when I heard my stairs squawking. I wasn't expecting any visitors at 2 AM. (Unfortunately.) I've shared my door key with a few close friends, so maybe someone had a bad night or something? Maybe needed to talk? A place to stay? Wouldn't they have called first? It was hard to be logical — my ears were still tugging at my brain to wake up.

Earlier in the night I thought I heard glass breaking. I knew I should get up. The cats probably knocked something over and I didn't want them to cut themselves. But I fell back asleep.

A guy appeared in my bedroom. Nope — nobody I knew. Wearing a jean jacket over a gray hooded sweatshirt, he calmly browsed my dresser. He picked something up. Adrenaline sparked under my skin like a flashbulb. I tried to sit up and clear my head.

"What are you doing?" I tried to bark in my toughest, deepest voice. But it came out with a yodel, "Wha ding?"

He grunted and hustled out, crunching down the noisy stairs. I flailed and kicked to untangle my feet from the sheets, then took up the chase. Halfway down the stairs, a familiar flapping reminded me I was naked. I ran back up and grabbed the only clothing handy: light blue boxer shorts decorated with cowboy lassos that spell out the word *Lucky*.

By then the thief had burst through the front door, across the yard and into the dark. As he escaped, he ditched the long, narrow box he had snatched from my dresser. It was the exact size of a necklace case, but instead held a dollar's worth of Nag Champa incense.

The flight down the stairs was enough to jump-start my brain. As I stood in the open doorway searching into the dark, I quickly weighed the wisdom of *heroic footchase* versus *running in my underpants down the street in the middle of the night*. I gathered up my incense and shuffled back inside.

I spent the rest of the evening waiting for the pumping adrenaline to fade. I fantasized about capturing the thief, about what I'd do if I caught him. But the imagery was hijacked by visions of me running in my underpants, making a diving catch and sliding across the concrete in my underpants, wrestling in my underpants, explaining the whole incident to the police while they took a mugshot of me in my Lucky Lasso cowboy underpants.

Somehow Superman looks fearsome in a blue leotard and Speedos. Maybe it's the way my underpants hang askew, or the spankety-spank sound my tender bare feet make when I run. For whatever reason, the lurking underworld did not quiver with fear that night.

I forgot I had a baseball bat near my bed for just such an occasion. Later, while running the whole event over in my mind, I picked up the bat and rehearsed how I might have wielded it. Standing on the narrow landing in my Lucky Lasso underpants, I discovered there wasn't room to swing the bat without taking out all the windows.

I want a pistol, but I know I'd use it for even the slightest infraction. "Get off my lawn!" *Blam!* "Newspaper's late!" *Blam!* "Your muffler's too loud!" *Blam!* So I bought a sling-shot, a fancy one that locks on your wrist. In the time it takes me to wrestle it on, fumble the BB into the pouch, drop the BB, dig around for it under the bed until I give up and get another one, take aim and then — *ow!* — step on the original BB, I could have gone to the pawn shop and bought back my stolen stuff. On the plus side, my ability to hit a target with a slingshot is about the same in pitch black as it is in broad daylight. When a giant ogre is lurking in your bedroom, the last thing you want to do is nick him with a pebble.

I settled on mace. I keep a handy little squirter by my bed. Unfortunately, I can't practice with it. If you spray the tiny can to see if it works, there might not be any left when you need it. So my fantasy of jumping up on my bed in my Superman underpants, taking aim with my chemical weapon and shouting, "Take *that,* villain!" is tempered by a nagging fear that I'll get nothing but a flaccid dribble of pepper jizz down my elbow.

I have an alarm system. So far, the score for setting it off is:

me = 328

burglars = 0.

I often hear phantom noises when I'm in the shower: voices, doorbells, phone ringing. I don't know why. Last week I heard a big thump. My cats devote their day to jacking around with everything, so thumps alone are not enough reason to run around wet and naked. But this was a *thump.* I paused to listen. Nothing, probably. A few creaks in a creaky old house. I took comfort because Phooey, our toothless old Shih Tzu, was undisturbed. Phooey barks when the neighbors open their garage door. He barks when icicles fall from the roof, and when the mail arrives. He was not barking now.

OF MICE AND ME

I reached for a towel and stepped gingerly out of the shower, still alert while quietly patting dry my shivering pink skin. Phooey exploded into wild barks, the *boo-woo-woo-woo* he picked up from watching the Three Stooges.

I never hear strange noises when I'm wearing a leather jacket and steel-toe boots while carrying a 10-inch chef knife. My heart sank as I dropped my towel and reached for my little sailboat underpants.

IN YOUR DREAMS

I awoke to what sounded like a nice dinner party: happy laughter, flirty conversation. My wife has the most engaging, infectious laugh, and I wondered uncomfortably who she was laughing with.

I felt like I was eavesdropping, the way you feel when someone is talking loudly into their cell phone. You'd like to give them some privacy if only you could figure out how. You can't very well dig a hole in the sidewalk and put your head in it. This psychological discordance is the basis for why we want to snatch the phone out of their hands and stomp it.

Her laugh came easily, her hands were animated. Clearly, she was having a lovely time, and clearly, she was dreaming. I hoped she would chuckle, "Oh, Michael, you're so clever," and feared I would hear her say, "Ha-ha-ha — oh, *Pierre*..."

Like looking into a Kleenex, where you know there's nothing good but you can't help yourself, I listened. I did not hear my name or anyone else's. Indeed, although her words were quite clear, I strained to recognize a single one of them. Perhaps she was enjoying a bistro lunch with Pierre. Or maybe dreams are coded to protect the dreamer.

Mercifully, it ended quickly. Why should I care? It's her dream, after all, and she's entitled to drift to all kinds of imaginary experiences, as long as she bathes herself in dream disinfectant afterwards. Thankfully, God alone is witness to the loopy stuff that goes on in my head at night. I don't choose any of it. I definitely didn't choose the terror of being locked in an Italian church dungeon, surrounded by gargoyles night after night. Maybe it's a nightmare for my wife to have wine at a sidewalk cafe in Paris with Pierre.

It's just as well I can't choose my dreams, because I'd stick to the same five or so, and enjoy them over and over, like Omaha radio does with music. At least with nightmares I have to get up and run occasionally.

Feeling bad about how I answered the following question, I posed it to my friends: "Who would you rather be: The good boyfriend a woman chooses to keep and trust and love? Or the bad boy she dumped as unworthy, but whom she secretly dreams about?" All hands shot up unanimously before I even finished the question: "Bad!" Male or female, every person but one answered the same way, and the one holdout was a liar. We'd rather be the one in the dream than the one in the bed.

A friend of mine was watching a romantic movie with her husband. The heroine on the screen writhed in ecstasy as a love scene played out in front of them. "I look like that to you," he asked tentatively, "don't I?"

"Yeah you do," she replied. "When I close my eyes."

GO FISH

I am dazzled by gear and distracted by shiny things, so you can imagine that I took to fishing like a fish to water. I could spend an hour watching the precise mechanism of a spinning reel methodically wind line onto its spool like a spider retracting a web.

I could stomach weaving a worm or leech onto a hook, but I never could bring myself to spear a minnow. Minnows have eyes, and a little Mr. Bill-shaped mouth.

As a little boy, it didn't bother me to catch fish in the Kearney Canal, which was a generous name for a ditch. My friend Harold and I would spend summer days crawling over the concrete chunks that buttressed the shoreline, eating cold beans out of a can and learning to lie. Carp would eat whatever garbage floated to the bottom, sucking crud off of miscellaneous junk that we, or generations of boys before us, thought would be hilarious to throw into the water. Amid that gunk, a worm probably looks good.

At some point, someone presented me with the notion of "catch-and-release." It is supposed to be humane and sporting, but it still involves piercing the fish's lip with a rusty hook and yanking it out of the water, except with catch-and-release you do it for no reason.

I imagined an alien landing on Earth, hooking me by the lip and dragging me kicking and screaming into his terrifying, ammonia-filled spaceship, then saying "Just kidding!" and turning me loose. The trouble with fishing is that once I start thinking, I ruin it.

Arthur, once my father-in-law, had a cabin in Minnesota where we'd vacation for a week each summer. It was expected of me to fish with Art every night. I'd bathe in DEET, pick out a pole from his formidable arsenal lined up like épées along the porch, and march dutifully to his 1950's-era pontoon boat. The deck was carpeted with AstroTurf, her frame made of rough steel that had been brush-painted royal blue. It looked like a floating football stadium and was just as nimble. We cast off at 8 PM, and the mosquitoes clocked in to work around 9.

Some folks think Minnesotans are joking about the size of their mosquitoes. Minnesquitoes really do cast a shadow. At dusk they swarm you in such a thick cloud that they obscure light. The drone of their wings sounds like a horror film soundtrack. Luckily the DEET in which I had marinated myself was as repugnant to them as it was to me, otherwise in seconds they'd have sucked me dry as a raisin.

I decided I liked going fishing. I just didn't like catching. Art would tell stories, and I'd nod and chuckle. Under the cover of darkness and behind the veil of mosquitoes I would skip baiting my hook. I'd simply enjoy the lazy repetition of casting and dragging my line through the water. Sometimes Art caught more fish than I did.

He normally caught walleye. It appears to me that all fish are wall-eyed. You never see one that is cross-eyed. One evening Art landed a wall-eyed pike. It fought viciously, and pike have razor-sharp teeth. If you could train pike, they'd be great for making a julienne of potatoes. But you can't train them, so they julienne whatever they want, including your fingers.

"Pick him up by the eyes," Art instructed. "It stuns 'em."

Picking up anybody by the eyeballs stuns them, thought. My imagination left behind its *fingers julienne* and took up being lifted by my eyeballs. I shook it off and grabbed the net.

As it happened, that was the last night of our vacation, so I didn't go fishing again that summer. As it happened, I was divorced the next spring, so as it happened I didn't go fishing again at all. But whenever I'm in a sporting goods store, I stop by the fishing section and admire the meticulous, intricate spinning reels. My imagination may have ruined fishing for me, but I still like the gear.

KEYS TO SUCCESS

One measure of the quality of my life is how many keys I have on my ring. Right now, I have four: front door, back door, garage door, car.

I hate keys. Keys remind me every day that people steal and I have to lock up my stuff. My hands full as usual, I curse as I fumble with keys to leave my house, to unlock my garage, unlock my car trunk, unlock my car. For good measure I curse the guy who stole my daughter's bicycle and made her cry — not because she lost her bike, but because it made her afraid I'd be mad at her, because she ached inside for an hour working up the courage to tell me. I *hate* him for that.

Not long ago I had a fat double-ring of keys, plus a set of "summer keys." They were my minimalist set: car key, house key. I used it when I went jogging or Frisbeeing or whatever, because I have no hips or butt and my regular wad of keys would pull down my shorts quicker than a junior high prankster.

It isn't entirely the fault of the heavy keys. These days I am shaped less like Big Man on Campus and more like Big Bird. This is why old men have their pants hiked up to their nipples. It's not a fashion choice, it's just the point at which their body tapers in enough for anything to grip on to.

When my key wad gets too big, I pause to examine my life to see why it has become so complicated. In spite of the mass of keys, in spite of the *Jingle Bells* song I make when I walk, I can't part with any of them. I need them just to manage my business: front door, back door, stock room, apartment doors, cash register, safe, garage, etc. *Sheesh.*

When the bar I owned was approaching its final lock-up, I expected to have moments of mixed emotions, second thoughts, sentimental memories, and such. To my surprise, every day seemed pretty much like a regular work day. Even though we had "last day open!" twice (thanks to the buyer's shady funding) I didn't really get *that feeling*.

Finally we closed the sale. Afterward I stopped by the bar to help one of the new guys get oriented. As I was finishing, it occurred to me that I should turn in my keys. I slowly unthreaded my "work" ring from my "life" ring,[29] and suddenly my softball-sized ball-and-chain shrunk down to just a few simple, lightweight keys. I felt naked. And like the naked, I felt liberated.

I walked slowly out the front door for the last time. Out of habit I called back, "Do you want me to lock you in?" realizing before I even finished that I no longer could. I couldn't come and go as I pleased. It was no longer my door.

That's when *that feeling* hit me.

---

29 I have systems for everything.

WHAT A DOLL

Happy Birthday, Barbie!

As I write this, she turned 57. She is eight days younger than I am. That makes her a Pisces: intuitive, creative, maybe a little aloof. Pisces are also prone to addictions and obsessive behavior, which you can tell just by looking at all her pink stuff.

She looks great though — far younger than her years — which often is the case with people who are injected full of plastic.

To mark that special day, oppressive paternal regimes banned Barbie altogether, including India, Saudi Arabia, the Taliban and West Virginia.

Barbie has been through a lot. As of today, she has had 108 occupations. It caused a media stir in 1995 when she was recalled from her Teacher Barbie job for not wearing underwear. She ran for President of the United States in 2004 as a member of the Girl Party.[30] For all her years, she has not found a job opportunity that doesn't require high heels.

According to Mattel, Barbie had a sister named Skipper, born in 1963, and Tutti, her twin, who came in 1964.[31] Both vanished years ago,

---

30 She lost.
31 I know, right? Imagine discovering you had an identical twin named Tutti. You'd have to wonder what your real first name had once been.

never to be seen again, primarily because nobody looked. Barbie got three new sisters thirty years later.

Including a horse, a lion cub and a chimpanzee, Barbie has had over fifty pets, not counting Ken. She and Ken, her boyfriend of forty years, broke up on Valentine's Day 2004 because he would not commit. Apparently she didn't count him dating her the previous forty years as commitment. They reunited in 2009. They are still not engaged.

If she were life-sized, she would be 6 feet tall, 100 pounds, a size 4, and her measurements would be 39-19-33. Her inventor, Ruth Handler, also held a patent on prosthetic plastic breasts for women, which were popular for having a very natural look and feel.

Barbie was named after the inventor's daughter, and Ken was named after the inventor's son. Give that a second thought.

Barbie was the first doll I wanted to undress. I had questions, and while I learned a lot, I ran into a few surprises years later when I encountered some missing details.

Parents can fly their children to Chicago to visit Barbie Place, where for $2200 (airfare included) you can have tea with your doll and get her hair styled. For about the same price, you can go to cosmetology school and style her hair yourself. There is also a Barbie Hospital, where you can replace broken limbs and heads, although not necessarily with matching ones. Body parts are expensive, so it is often cheaper to get a new Barbie than it is to Frankenstein one together out of spare parts. That is the only thing Barbie and real people have in common.

So happy birthday, Barbie. I wish you fifty more fascinating years. And good luck with that Ken thing.

IF YOU WANT MY ADVICE

VOTING SIGNS

We just finished an odd election year. Omaha elections are odd in general. Always.

We vote for Omaha mayor and all seven city council seats in odd numbered years, the first year after a presidential election, on the first Tuesday after the second Monday in May. This is to help make sure our front yards are always filled with flimsy red and blue signs like a bloom of spring dandelions, even in off years.

Last election offered a stark choice among the two mayoral candidates: one a meeting-lover, one a pile-driver. The first a consensus-builder, the other a procedural independent. She'll let you know what she did after she did it.

Statistically, it was a tight race. Five percent of voters strongly favored one candidate or the other, twenty percent were undecided, and seventy five percent didn't know there was an election.

It boils down to this: one candidate doesn't care what you think; she already knows what she wants to do. The other candidate needs to call a meeting to find out what *he* thinks. It was a hard choice.

After that I decided to create a voter guide that's universal, so we don't have to start from scratch every year. We need—

Wait! Did I say *universal*? What a great idea! Why don't we leave it to astrology to decide how we should vote? Let's try it: just look up your sign that follows, and let the stars be your guide.

~ ASTROLOGY TIP SHEET ~

Aries: You are bright, dynamic, quick-witted and impatient. You will vote early and choose the first person on the list, just to get it over with.

Taurus: You are determined, efficient, stubborn, and conservative. You will be on your hands and knees in your yard pulling weeds when you realize you were supposed to vote yesterday.

Gemini: You are lively, social, literary and communicative. You will read all of one candidate's treatises and attend all of the neighborhood chats and town halls of the other. Then you will flip a coin.

Cancer: You are emotional, sensitive, moody and conscientious. Voting is important to you. You will have pencil in hand on your way to the voting booth when someone invites you to a party. Oh heck — you can't pass up a party.

Leo: You are extroverted, dignified, proud, a lover of the limelight and a natural leader. You don't care about this race because you are not in it.

Virgo: Practical, responsible, a careful planner and a dedicated perfectionist. You can't vote because you're a volunteer poll worker.

Libra: You are idealistic, diplomatic, fair-minded, and indecisive. You'd rather not choose one, because you don't want to make the other candidate feel like a loser.

Scorpio: You are intense, powerful, strong-willed, and rebellious. You won't vote for one candidate because he pissed you off fifteen years ago and you don't forget stuff like that. The other's out because you think he's a sissy and you hate sissies. You'll write in the name of one of your friends.

Sagittarius: You are idealistic, optimistic, freedom-loving and gregarious. It's only the mayoral race — how much harm can he do? You skip voting and go for a bike ride in the sun.

Capricorn: You are ambitious, disciplined, thrifty, and responsible. I wish you were running. Vote for yourself.

Aquarius: You are individualistic, unconventional, independent, and unpredictable. Like *I'm* supposed to figure out who you'll vote for?

Pisces: You are supersensitive, impressionable, sympathetic, and intuitive. The first candidate is good because he has all that experience, but he also made a lot of enemies along the way, y'know? The other gets along pretty well with everybody, but that's only because he tries so hard to please and doesn't really take a stand of his own. But that can be a good thing too, since he'll respond to the consistuents, don't you think? Listening is important, and it's good to have a consensus. But *dude,* sooner or later a guy has to take a stand, right? And pick a side? You can't just gather opinions all day, or you'll never—what's that? The poll closed?

YOU SAY YOU WANT AN EVOLUTION

So the president's opinion on gay marriage is *evolving*. He had strong opinions one way, now maybe he's swinging the other way, so to speak. I know better to jump into that discussion, so... [jump!]

He chooses his words carefully. *Evolving* is not the same as *changing*. To evolve is to develop new characteristics ever so slowly, so slowly you can't even see it happen, but in time you discover you've become distinctly different. You *change* your mind. You *evolve* a new head.

So probably he didn't change his mind. Probably he's trying hard to make baby steps because everyone around him wants him to. He *has* to evolve. But we'll never know, will we?

Evolution is like that. We never know. For all the arguments about the science of species evolution [jump!] there really isn't any evidence of it. Darwin had no "theory of evolution." He proposed only that better-adapted animals were more likely to breed, which explains why Andy Warhol didn't have kids. There's plenty of evidence for birds changing colors or dogs breeding floppier skin, but there's no evidence of birds turning into dogs. The familiar illustration of hunchy little monkeys growing taller and straighter is fine until they turn into a human in a pinstripe suit. Maybe it happened that way, but no one has any evidence of it.

Then, of course, if monkeys evolved into humans, why are there still monkeys? Monkeys live without destroying their environment. They engage each other in an endlessly sustainable existence. If anything, humans should evolve into chimps.

Only God knows. As people are quick to point out, I am not a god. If I were — if I could steer evolution — I'd make these changes:

Eyeballs should be mounted on the end of fingers. That way you could look over high shelves, spy over fences, see where your keys fell under the car seat, and get a better look at your bald spot and that mole on your butt. Hammering a nail would require a little extra courage. Without eye sockets, our head could grow into one solid bony helmet to protect our precious brain.

Our nose would be better served on our fingertips too, so we could figure out where that stink is coming from without all the stooping. So I guess my future human would be just a bunch of sense organs at the end of his arms — a radar array anemone hand.

Testicles dangling front and center, bouncing back and forth in a thin skin bag like two kids conking heads in the back seat of a car on a bumpy road — whose idea was that? If balls are so important, shouldn't they be tucked safely inside? Like inside the brain?[32] Where they wouldn't be a bulls-eye for every baseball? Where we wouldn't have to see them? Eyeballs are surrounded by protective bone, yet our reproductive future dangles out there as fragile as Fabergé eggs.

Physiologists (and people in general) marvel at the way testicles rise and fall like a yo-yo (okay, two yo-yos), to coddle our temperature-sensitive sperm. Isn't that *genius?* Humans can control the temperature

---

32 Testicles closer to the brain would surely have other benefits too.

of an office tower with a twist of a thermostat. Women have managed to keep their eggs tucked safely inside for years. Maybe women are just more evolved.

Fauna is full of variety: gills, feathers, fingers, spines. But there's also a curious consistency: almost all animals have a nose. Two eyes. Not one, not three. Appendages appear in pairs, even though a tripod would be far more stable — just ask a kangaroo. Did God intentionally restrict himself to a palette of building blocks like Legos, from which he could build anything, but everything would look like *he* built it?

Did a giraffe grow a long neck so he could eat leaves higher on a tree, or does he eat leaves high on a tree because he has a long neck? Maybe Adam and Eve were plopped onto this Earth as two beautiful, fully-formed 30-year-old adults, their tender feet nestled in soft green grass. But if they were born perfect, we definitely didn't evolve for the better.

WITH FRIENDS LIKE THESE

"You unfriended me."

"No I didn't."

"You did. We were Facebook friends and now we're not."

We're still friends. We were always friends. *Facebook friends* aren't friends. They are connections. They are the people you can spam when you have no real friends to whine to.

When you start a rant about how you hate the government, or how many assault rifles you deserve, or how you don't understand why people eat raw fish, or why Prince is the *best musician ever*, do you see those real humans around you who smile politely, clear their throats and change the subject? Those are your real friends. They care about you enough to help you not be a jackass.

In spite of what Facebook says, you do not have 1,485 friends.

When you and your Facebook friends all change your Facebook profile photo into your favorite Munster's character to show support for Serbian refugees, the real refugees are still real refugees.

You wouldn't mail real postcards to your real friends announcing what you found behind the pig pen in your game of BarnVille, but your Facebook friends will give you a virtual egg in congratulations. They'll watch with envy for two seconds as you become the mayor of Grounds Zero Coffee Shop. They tolerate your real estate posts because they want to send you their band announcements.

Facebook has ruined high school reunions. I no longer have any reason to go home and find out how my classmates turned out, catch up on what they're doing these days, hear what offensive opinions they hold, see how fat they got. Facebook gives us hourly updates, reminding us why we left town in the first place.

I deleted you from my Facebook list after you posted five rants in a row containing angry, spitty, narrow-minded stuff you'd never say out loud, and you only typed it because you were home alone and drunk. I didn't "unfriend" you. I stopped listening to your crap.

I'm still your friend.

Facebook friends send you *hugs!* when you post that you are "feeling sad" at 2 AM. They give you a *thumbs up!* when you are "ready to face Monday!" *Thumbs up!* when you are defiant about pretty much anything. *Thumbs up!* when you want to recall the mayor, even though you haven't thought for fifteen seconds who you might like to replace her. *Thumbs up!* that you oppose cancer.

For years *thumbs up!* was the only response available on Facebook. Your Facebook friends are 100% thumbs up. No thumbs down. No middle finger.

When you announce that your cat died, your Facebook friends *are sending our thoughts and prayers to you and your family,* when actually they skipped on to a video of a squirrel running around in traffic with a plastic cup stuck on his head.

Facebook is there for you when you feel alone. It supports every notion that blips out of your fingers. It always *likes!* you.

I, on the other hand, am your friend.

ANY OTHER DAY

We don't call it World Trade Center Day. Or the Twin Towers Attack. Or the al-Qaeda Massacre. (Maybe because we wouldn't know *which* massacre.) We obliquely refer to it as "The Events of September 11."

It isn't even "event*s*," unless you count each plane separately.

Event? A half-price sale is an event. A family reunion is an event. Intentionally crashing four airliners loaded with innocent passengers on a sunny autumn morning, killing 3000 people, is bigger than an event—try *carnage, genocide,* or *slaughter.*

Like Memorial Day, D-Day, and Independence Day, The Events of September 11 saw heroes leap into action. Others froze in confusion and fear, still more went about their business telling themselves, "If I act like nothing is happening, then this will all just go away." I usually end up in that third group.

I've always thought of New York City as being the fount of creativity. It is a city of writers, and home to nearly every major publishing and advertising house. So this attack on its heart, and the unfortunate moniker of Ground Zero as the location — isn't it time we honor it with a real name?

To be fair, just a month after the attack, Congress rushed to declare September 11 Patriot Day by a vote of 407–0. Twenty-five members didn't vote. I'd have been in that group too. Maybe it didn't stick because *patriot* is a little general for this application: it doesn't refer to what happened that day at all. The biggest act of patriotism at the time was to insist on referring to French fries as Freedom fries.[33] Or maybe it was because Patriot's Day was already a holiday in Massachutsetts, Maine and Wisconsin, celebrating the start of the American Revolution. (Patriots indeed!) Since they get Monday off, folks there enjoy a three-day weekend, and people remember that sort of thing. It's also a holiday in Quebec to honor, specifically, patriots.

Fourth of July isn't so far from being called The Events of July 4, but at least it has a real name: Independence Day. I guess we don't call it Independence Day much because "4th" is easier to spell.

Nobody refers to D-Day as The Events of June 6. That legendary day is also called Operation Overlord, and even Operation Neptune. Those are swell names, befitting the courage of everyone involved. If June 6 deserves three names, September 11 should at least get one.

Can you imagine buying presents to celebrate The Events of December 25? Not to compare myself to the baby Jesus, but I was The Event of March 1.

What if something else happens on September 11? Are we going to call it *One* of The Events? We honor Christopher Columbus on Columbus Day, Martin Luther King Jr. on Martin Luther King Jr. Day, and the death of Jesus on Good Friday (although I don't see what was so good about it). We celebrate the death of good taste on St. Patrick's Day, and on Memorial Day we celebrate the death of just about everyone else. We don't celebrate the deaths of American legends John Adams, James Monroe or Theodore Roosevelt because they all died on July 4th. "Sorry, you can't have July 4th. It's already the 4th of July."

How about the guy who presents an engagement ring to his girlfriend on her birthday? It's a classic male maneuver to duck out of

---

33 At the time we forgot the French helped us win our own freedom during the Revolutionary War.

gift shopping—a two-for-one. He considers *himself* the present. He hijacks her birthday and doubles it down into their anniversary too. But now he is doomed to forget it. He'll dilute her birthday every year for the rest of their marriage. Just ask anyone whose birthday is on New Year's Eve.

Calling it The Events of September 11 has little connection to the tragedy itself, unless you argue that the towers were shaped like an 11. New Yorkers: you love to tell us where you were when it happened, especially those of you who were *there* when it happened. I challenge you to put your legendary creativity to work on this one: come up with a mighty name to honor that terrifying, disorienting, surreal attack, so it isn't named like any other day.

A NIGHT AT THE OPERA

The first thing I noticed about the opera was that the entire theater staff was smiling. From the elderly doorman in his braided jacket that looked like it came from the closet of Michael Jackson, to the ticket takers beaming as if their kids were in the show, smiles were everywhere.

The next thing I noticed was that tickets were $120. That explained the grins.

The Orpheum Theater in Omaha is a splendid venue, one of seven ornate sisters originally built for the vaudeville circuit. It is resplendent in velvet, gilded in sweeping gold arches, and has a chandelier the size of a bread truck. If I paid $5 for a show and the performers didn't show up, I'd still feel I got my money's worth just craning my head at the magnificenct lobby.

Grinning ushers herded us to our seats. It was in my favorite section, the narrow side of the loge, where there's extra velvet and gilding and you can look down on the floor people. We were right behind the box seats, so I kept looking over my shoulder and imagining, if anyone started shooting, how I might save the president.

The only person who needed shooting that night was the old lady right behind me. The minute *The Marriage of Figaro* began and the cast started bellowing and hiding behind chairs, she began uncrinkling candy. It is a miracle of acoustics that a candy wrapper can drown out a professional opera singer. For whatever reason, ladies unwrap candy as slowly as if it were given to them in a concentration camp and they had to live off it for a week. I have never seen anybody, young or old, eat hard candy outside a theater.

Maybe it wasn't candy. After ten minutes of slow, piercing crinkling, I began to suspect she was making cellophane origami gifts for all of her grandchildren. I turned around a couple of times to give her the Midwestern faux-polite look, a blend of "How do you do?" and "I'm about to fling you off the balcony." She might as well have been engrossed in her knitting, since she didn't react to me at all. Perhaps she was knitting cellophane mittens.

Being a Midwesterner, I seethed to myself and never actually said any real words. During intermission, after pretty much everyone in the cast had taken a turn hiding behind the chair on stage, we snuck up to the unused box seats in front of us, long on leg room and short on crinkling. I always think of John Wilkes Booth when I sit up there, knowing that at the Orpheum he would not have jumped on stage shouting *"Sic semper tyrannis!"* but instead would crash deep into the orchestra pit among the percussionists, where he belonged.

This was my first time seeing *The Marriage of Figaro*. I speak a little Italian, so I'm pretty sure nobody got married, although I confess I nodded off a couple of times in the third hour. I also concluded that nobody in that performance had any business even considering marriage, not until they made up their minds whom they were in love with.

I was surprised at how young the conductor was. He appeared to be a high school senior. With talent beyond his years, his hands swept in graceful waves and his baton speared the air. The orchestra, in perfect unison, ignored him.

The musicians were arranged by attitude. The French horn players, according to tradition, were all wearing flannel shirts. The oboists all wore expressions that said they had just argued about Nietzsche and lost. The flutists were predictably slender and pretty, erect in posture, blissfully above the raging battle over whether they should be called *flautists*.

I knew the opera would be three hours long. I check details like that before agreeing to attend, ever since I was ambushed by a four-hour performance of *Madame Butterfly*, which was fat with madames but not one butterfly. The performance was special because a famous local ceramicist, known for making giant spotted eggs, had been convinced to try his hand at costuming. When a big lady draped in a muumuu with large black spots sang, I suddenly craved Ben & Jerry's.

Soon came the moment I was waiting for. My dear friend appeared on stage. He was among the chorus members, handsome in his dramatic blue-black ponytail. Other ponytails in the cast looked like they came off a Paul Revere costume. His rich baritone swelled to fill the open space as he moved with the confidence of Keanu Reeves.

The entire cast was fit and trim. The only lady remotely pudgy had not sung a note in twenty minutes, so it caught me off guard when the opera ended.

We lingered a bit after the show, admiring the elegant surroundings. The ushers spread out in a dragnet of black uniforms linked across the aisles. Their smiles sagged into the tight grimace of FBI agents. They swept us up and ushered us out.

"Wait," I said to my wife as we stepped into the cold air, away from the lobby and toward a martini. "I never heard *Feeeg-ahhhh-roooh! Figaro-Figaro-Figaro-Figaro-Feeeg-ahhhh-roooh.*"

"That's *The Barber of Seville*," she replied. "Rossini. This was Mozart. *Marriage of Figaro*."

"Oh." After a few more steps I asked, "So *The Barber of Seville* is the one with the rabbit?"

"Yep."

How does opera always find a way to make me feel stupid?

DON'T CALL ME RICH

I heard the hundredth interview with someone who lost his fortune to Bernie Madoff. The man complained viciously that now, after years of careful planning, he might be forced to work.

I tried to be sympathetic. Let's say you had a baby bunny rabbit and kept it for years on your plush red velour couch, and fed it only milk and bon-bons its whole life. Then suddenly you cast it into the woods to fend for itself. Something like that.

The more the interviewer listened, the more Mr. Bunny ranted and raged. After wishing death by starvation upon Mr. Madoff and his family, the man went on to blame the U.S. government, demanding reimbursement. I suppose that's because Madoff doesn't have any money, and the government does. It was tax time after all, and the government seemed to be reimbursing a lot of people. Mr. Bunny's voice was rising to the range where only bats could hear him as he sprayed the microphone with spit.

The interviewer asked him if he had ever met Mr. Madoff. "No," he replied, "and now I don't want to." He had never set eyes on the man, but gave him $250 million dollars. Stupid government.

According to my investment history, I could do better with your money than Bernie. If I could get a complete stranger to give me $250 million, I bet I would only lose half of it.

Here's the part I can't get over: if I had $250 million dollars, and I lost $249 million, I'd *still have one million dollars*.

I understand Mr. Bunny not wanting to get a job. I've been unemployed before, and was never happier. I know people get rich without jobs, so I went to the internet to find out how I could do that too. I looked up the keywords *Get Rich No Job*. It looks like most opportunities are in telemarketing, envelope stuffing, and investment brokering.

I was accidentally invited to a dinner party hosted by a prominent lawyer. An attractive young drunk woman in a sequined dress, which was trying to slip away from her just like everyone else, drug herself up to me and gurgled, "Are you rich?"

"Nope. I'm Michael." *Ba-da-boom.*

Nice," she slurred as she raised her champagne glass at my face, then slithered, eyes half-open, off to the next guy.

Nice indeed, I thought. My relative poverty saved the day. Maybe I'll thank the government.

DO IT IN DUBAI

Warren Buffett is among the richest men in the world. Except for playing the ukulele, he doesn't appear to be having much fun with his money. We in Nebraska love him for that. Midwesterners are known for helping you up if you suffer misfortune, and if you suffer a lot of fortune, we'll chip you back down. We put great value on mediocrity.

The fun of being rich is doing things other people can't afford to do. That's hard when everyone around you is rich too. Los Angeles is among the toughest places to be rich. Look what Michael Jackson had to go through to stand out.

The hardest place of all to look rich? Dubai — *everybody* there is rich. So how can you look richer than the rich in Dubai?

One guy built a ski resort.

First he built a full-sized mountain, then put a building over it, and made it cold enough inside that it snowed every day. Dubai is made of sand because it's too hot and dry for dirt to survive. In Nebraska we don't cherish snow so much — indeed, we'd be happy to export it to any of the Arab Emirates — but it's not about the snow. It's about snow *in Dubai*, a land so hot and dry that you brush your teeth with steam.

Outer space was supposed to be the next frontier. The rich guys at Virgin are already taking reservations for regular commercial trips to space. But the crazy rich are not yet sold on building vacation homes out there, because there are no poor people up there to envy them. That spoils the fun of blowing money. Until someone builds really cheap, really powerful telescopes so the rest of us can watch the rich float and tumble and try to go swimming in weightless wonder, they'll have to be ostentatious a little closer to home.

My friend Skye skidded up to us, arms waving, as we sat at the bar. "Ohmygod-ohmygod-oh my *god!*" she yelled without introduction. "The next big thing: underwater."

We've learned not to interrupt Skye when she gets like this. "People are going to start building fancy houses *underwater.* Oceans are the new suburbs!"

Maybe she's right. It's hard to resist watching underwater films of dolphins and octopuses and other sea magicians. We proletariat can't afford to live underwater, but our imaginations would bubble over watching some rich Hefner dude throw an underwater dinner party in his underwater house, everyone fitted with black velvet oxygen tanks. We'd *oooh* and *aaah* as a romantic couple drifted away from the dinner crowd to enjoy the balcony view and an extra dry martini, as their hair wafted dramatically in the current. Later, someone could strum an underwater guitar as they gathered around the underwater fireplace. Perhaps a midnight dip in the underwater swimming pool.

Skye thinks ahead. "Imagine how much it would cost to get a FedEx delivery to your underwater house!" I hadn't imagined that. "You'd have to buy a new *everything!* An underwater pet. Underwater furniture. An underwater hair dryer that blows really hot water."

The rich folk would lose their desire to swim in the regular ocean, because — heck, any schmoe can do that.

To look rich in Nebraska, all you have to do is hire a housekeeper and a lawn service. *Gasp!* But for the poor rich people in Dubai, the only impressive step left will be to build a giant artificial ocean above ground, right above the desert sand, so passers-by can be dazzled by your underwater extravagance as they shuffle by on their way to the plain old ski lift.

SPACE-AGE TECHNOLOGY

I can't remember the last time I felt bored.

As a kid I would get bored every day. Eventually I would dream up something to amuse myself, after my mind had idled so long that it hallucinated itself into a creative frenzy. I'd go outside and build dirt roads for my Tonka trucks in a city featuring a stray-cat hotel, or assign names to the ants and test myself to remember who was who. Sometimes I'd just dig a hole, in case I ever needed one.

The first computer I ever saw was a Commodore 64: a tiny, inexpensive unit that had to be programmed by hand every time you turned it on, because floppy drive storage hadn't been invented yet. Once you took the time to learn the computer's language, you could switch it alive and, with only about twenty minutes of coding, instruct it to take over your TV and display in ominous green letters:

"*My name is Michael.*

Run again? (Y)es, (N)o."

All this computer programming saved me the time of having to type, "My name is Michael," although actually I did have to type it because it was part of the program code. With a tweak, you could create an endless loop so it would print your message, repeating line after line, so fast it became a flickering conveyor belt of egotism. Such an arrangement would definitely be faster than me hand-typing it over and over indefinitely. When encountering a demo computer in a store, I'd type in my sentence (or something a little racier) and run away giggling, as if I had just started War Games.

As cell phones grew in popularity, I blossomed into a Luddite. I resisted the idea of callers being able to reach me wherever I was. I was satisfied with the aloofness of my answering machine, which solved the quandary of how to avoid certain people while not missing out on anything fun.

Eventually I did get a cell phone, after convincing myself that I'd use it only to make calls for emergencies like ordering pizza so I could pick it up on my way home. I'd share my number only with a chosen few. I stored the numbers of all my favorite fast-food restaurants and people so I could drunk-dial them.

My first cell phone was a Nokia: black, leather-bound and as big as a Three Musketeers bar.[34] It had a one-inch screen and the sound was scratchy. The first emergency my new phone encountered was when I dropped it at a music festival and it was run over by a hearse.

My current cell phone is the size of a candy bar now, which is to say, unsatisfying. It looks like a candy bar too, a bite-sized black rectangle with rounded corners, and just as slippery. If I try to wedge it between my ear and shoulder when I need to use my hands for other things, it squirts out like a pumpkin seed.

Cell phones save time by keeping us constantly connected. Driving time can now double as chat time with friends, and we get home sooner because while we were checking our text messages we drove through all the red lights.

---

34 A 1995 candy bar was big.. Candy bars have shrunk over time just as much as cell phones.

OF MICE AND ME

My computer checks for e-mail messages every fifteen minutes. In between, I usually push the "Mail" button to make it check again, because e-mail is way more fun than working. Think of all the paper and postage I'm saving by not using regular mail to forward jokes and kitten pictures to all my friends.

Today, rather than going to all the trouble of dialing ten whole digits in a row and speaking to someone, we hand-type messages using our opposable thumbs. I'm beginning to suspect this is why monkeys got rid of theirs. I've mentioned before that I support the idea of evolution, but we probably have the direction wrong. Monkeys live happily in the tropics, eat fresh food for free, don't need jobs, pet each other's hair, and when they need to communicate over long distances, they holler. Instead of forwarding each other memes and watching porn videos, they take naps and have actual sex.

Typing with thumbs is technology going backwards, not forwards. The next generation of smart phone will probably require us to communicate by pounding it against a rock in Morse Code.

We've come almost full-circle. My newest phone lets me talk into it, and it transcribes my words into text, which I edit because it turned "I'm on my way home" into "I monitor Wyoming." With a single button push after a bunch of button pushes to chose my recipient, it delivers my text to you at the speed of light. If you have a fancy phone like mine, it will read the text aloud using one of four voices, none which sounds like me.

Imagine the possibilities! Someday maybe I'll be able to speak into my phone and you could literally hear *me* from wherever you are!

Here's my suggestion for a new mobile device: the cell toilet. "Look! They're so small and light you can take one with you wherever you go! Relieve yourself while you walk! Even while you drive! Eventually you'll get rid of your old land toilet. These are so cheap you won't even care if it quits working. Just throw it away and buy another!"

"It's a paper cup."

"That's the beauty of it! It's recyclable. It'll even reduce your water bill! Think of the time you'll save: you can use it while chatting *and* driving!"

What I really want is a big, sturdy, comfortable phone that gets great reception, one with big luxurious speakers that fit warmly against my ear, and a mouthpiece that reaches all the way to my mouth. Something indestructible, heavy enough that I can slam it down hard when I hang up on a telemarketer or ex-girlfriend. One that doesn't require recharging, yet lasts for years. I want a real Space Age kind of phone — which is to say, one from the 1960s.

THIS JOB BLOWS

It was embarrassing to fire up my snowblower this morning. Total snow accumulation would hardly bury a penny. Little came out the chute; it looked more like wispy steam. But still, it felt faster than pushing a shovel all over, and I love power tools.

To justify myself, I buzzed my neighbor's sidewalk too. Brian has a real job and actually goes to work. I thought about doing his driveway too but decided circling his house unexpectedly might give his wife and kids the creeps.

My total invested time was about twenty seconds. Shortly after, their fine, handsome son Sam appeared at my door with a full plate of homemade chocolate chip cookies. He looked as perplexed as I was. Their total invested time: one hour. My breezy little gesture became a windfall. I wondered whether if I washed their car they'd paint my house.

Americans are the only culture in the world that considers a gift to be a social burden. Someone sent you a Christmas card? *Dang it!* Now you have to send them one in return. You rush outside in the sleet to shop for one so you can get it in the return mail before Christmas.

We have to defend ourselves against gifts, lest we are tattooed with a big scarlet *D* for *Deadbeat*. If not yourself, you know someone who buys and wraps an extra gift or two just in case some weirdo shows up at the last minute with a present. "Why, I was just about to bring this over," you'll lie. "You saved me a trip!" It's the Strategic Gift Defense System.

Salami is perfect for this application: it keeps forever since it's not really food, and yet it has the air of, "Hey, I just whipped this up!" If someone gives you one of those Hillshire Farms gift boxes, with salami and warm greasy cheese, some random jelly thing, and those unmarked cellophane-wrapped hard candies made in China, all snuggled in fake grass as if a chicken just laid it all, you can toss it on top of the fridge and re-present it when needed. It's the aikido of gifts.

Some people just duck their friends, as if gift-giving was akin to being served a warrant. If they can't find you to give a gift, you don't have to give one back. Plus, it's one more excuse to stay inside and watch TV all day.

The U.S. is one of the only countries where it's not rude to give a tit-for-tat gift. In many countries the best way to honor a gift is to pass it off to someone else. The better the gift, the farther it goes. In America, if I gave you an iPad and you immediately tossed it to the person behind you, I'd freak out. "Hey, give it back then!"

I'll keep blowing my neighbor's snow just to see how long before he throws open the window and yells, *"Knock it off, jackass!"*

OF MICE AND ME

THE IWISH

It's about the size of an Etch-A-Sketch, but without the big white knobs. It is named after a pad of paper, but it doesn't come with a pencil. That's progress.

The iPad, Apple's must-have internet device, claims to do everything with nothing. It doesn't have a keyboard. You type on *pictures* of letters, which feels a bit like drumming your fingers in boredom.

Apple founder Steve Jobs called the iPad a "window to the internet." Any window to the internet ought to come with shutters, but the iPad doesn't have those either. It runs all of the popular iPhone apps, those little programs that are cheap or free and entertain you as well as anything cheap or free. Maybe someone will develop an app for the iPad that is a picture of shutters, so I can block out upsetting internet images of violence, porn, and Glenn Beck.

The iPad does look a little like a window. It's a square frame surrounding a picture of rolling hills, with icons neatly arranged along the bottom, waiting for you to clutter them up with real work. You hold the iPad up to look through it and see whatever you want, like Miss Linda on Romper Room with her Magic Mirror. She saw Billy and Sarah and Tommy and Julie, but no matter how much I waved my hands in front of the TV, she never saw Mickey. At least the iPad includes face recognition software.

The iPad is the latest time-saving convenience, and like all time-savers before it, I'll spend eighty percent of my day playing games and checking Facebook to discover what everybody is making for dinner. Since I got my iPhone, my regular job has waited patiently while I practice my air traffic skills, frantically guiding home plane after plane until one crashes into another in a game ironically named Flight Control. I presume a real air traffic controller gets fired when two jetliners collide at the head of a runway, so my career lasts about two minutes. I estimate that as of today, I have killed 23,000 passengers. An iPad's large screen would make room for bigger planes.

I would buy an iPad — I adore everything Apple makes — but I haven't had any money since I bought my iPhone. I know the iPhone, which I lusted for like a boy over a Daisy Air Rifle, would be tossed aside in the iPad's skinny shadow, to gather dust just like my once-cherished iPod, which is now a $200 coaster.

For the new iPad to improve my life, it needs to include these apps:

- *iSlouch,* a free app that counts the calories I'm not burning anymore.
- *iStrain,* a mirror app that reflects my own burned-red eyes, dried out from not blinking as I crash another 747 into an Airbus 380.
- *SkeeDaddle,* an app that predicts the approach of the repo man.

America needs a better internet fantasy device because internet reality is so disappointing. A *real* reality show would include an hour-long YouTube video of me with a mouth full of Wheat Thins, slumped over an iPad like a mother over a newborn.

So far, there's no app for that.

BREAK A LEG

Laura is an actress, and she scored a great part in a significant play. Big stage, good role, full house. Friends lined up to wish her, "Good luck!"

"Aaagh! *Never* say 'good luck' to an actor!" she'd reply with wide-eyed alarm while tossing salt over her shoulder. "It's bad luck! Always say, 'break a leg.'"

"Sorry," the friend would reply, sorry mostly that he wished her good luck in the first place.

"Break a leg" is a superstition I haven't parsed yet. Tradition or not, saying "break your leg" to Laura is like telling my daughters, "I hope you knock out a tooth!"

Some say the tradition started with John Wilkes Booth, a famous actor back then and a famouser assassin now, who snapped his ankle while unsuccessfully jumping from the elegant box seats of the Ford Theater after successfully shooting Abraham Lincoln in the back of the head. Most of us wouldn't wish him good luck in any form and are glad he broke a leg.

If any advice was to be gleaned from Booth, it was "Don't hide in a barn full of flammable hay!" Or, "*Our American Cousin?* Wait for it to come out on DVD!" But that takes too long to say. We prefer something snappy. "Break a leg" has a nice ring to it. Actors know a good hook when they hear one.

The French/Spanish/Portuguese wish each other "lots of *merde/mierda/merda!*" Shit. *"Merde!"* is also a worldwide good luck wish in ballet. It is bad luck to wish a broken leg on a ballerina.

The theoretical origins of "break a leg" are too numerous to list, and they all sound like stories made up by actors.

Actors have more superstitions than anyone, even pitchers. Actors think they'll learn a script better if they put it under their pillow while they sleep. I tried that for junior high algebra class. Sleeping over *Cliff's Notes* worked about as well, which is to say not at all, but I slept in half the time.

A bad dress rehearsal means a good opening night. Maybe just in comparison.

Peacock feathers are never allowed on stage, even as a prop. This superstition was probably started by peacocks.

Actors never use real money on stage. That's no surprise. Actors never use real money anywhere.

Green is an unlucky color for actors. This is because performances used to be staged outdoors, and actors did not want to be confused with bushes. Unless, of course, they are playing a bush.

I once witnessed a rehearsal where, at the end of the reading, the entire troupe turned and glared at one hapless member. I learned an actor is never to utter the last line of the play until the audience is in attendance. To everyone's astonishment, the building did not burn down. Not right then, anyway.

Never mention or quote *Macbeth* while in a theater. The play is cursed. They used real witches for the first production. That turned out as badly as their decision to use real swords in the fight scenes. The show *Mystery Hunters* tested the Curse of Macbeth by walking around in a theater whispering "Macbeth!" Nothing happened, unless you count their show being cancelled.

OF MICE AND ME

Actors always leave one light on in an empty theater. It's called the "ghost light." This practice has spread to society in general, as we all believe it is bad luck to stumble around a cluttered room full of trap doors in the dark.

Theaters are always closed one night a week to allow ghosts to perform their own play. Usually it is a Monday. No one has ever witnessed a ghost performance, probably because it is hard to get people out on a Monday night.

So "good luck" is bad luck. My dad took that cue and would say the opposite of what he wished for to make things come true. "Don't get a real job!" "Don't go back for your MBA!"

ON HOLIDAY

A YEAR OF EATING DANGEROUSLY

Before we buttered our first roll, before the glasses were filled with milk, before we even had a chance to say grace, my mother set down the platter of turkey and announced the Thanksgiving ground rules: "Everybody — save the neck for Dad."

There was a pause as our eyes darted back and forth. Nobody has ever asked less of a child. It was the only time the six of us kids had ever been in complete agreement. Mom might as well have instructed us to save him the eyeballs.

Vultures eat disgusting things, things that would poison a human. Their intestines have a chemical make-up which allows the most vile rot to be edible. When vultures pick over a dead carcass, they skip the neck.

Normally, it was fun to watch Dad eat, because he always had a tiny bit of corn stuck on his chin — even if we weren't having corn. But the thought of him baring his magnificent false teeth, tugging away at some gristly rope of neck to tear off a stretchy morsel of purple meat like Tom Hanks in *Big* eating the little baby ear of corn? No thanks.

To be fair, I've never tasted turkey neck. I've only seen one peripherally through my squinted, averted eyes. Store-bought turkeys don't come with necks anymore.

A few random organs are still included, neatly gift-wrapped and nestled inside the bird — probably not from that bird originally, but that's not a big issue for those people who feel they're owed some organs. But there has been no outcry at the absence of the neck.

Thanksgiving turkey itself is probably on its last legs, so to speak. I heard this a lot last year: "I just don't like turkey." It had never occurred to me that liking turkey was an option at Thanksgiving.

A lot of cooks wouldn't care if we skipped turkey altogether. Thanksgiving is the only time most of us handle a dead body the size of a three-year-old.

Party food stopped making sense about the time pioneers stopped wearing buckles on their hats. Stuffing, for example, requires stale bread, which we don't have anymore. Bread no longer goes stale because it is no longer made of food. I bought a loaf of raisin bread last March, and by October it was still good. Even mold won't eat it.

To make stale bread, you have to drive around in your car hanging it out the window. Or be a real American: go buy stale bread at the store. You can buy a can of stale bread crumbs for only three times the cost of fresh bread.

Valentine's Day has much better holiday food. Any menu is fine, really, as long as it includes chocolate. The problem is that the Valentine's Day dinner isn't followed by a football game on TV. After steak and seafood in a rich butter sauce with a bottle of wine, finished with chocolate mousse and a ruby-red port, you are expected to be romantic.

The opposite of good holiday food is St. Patrick's Day. Corned beef and boiled cabbage are two reasons the Irish fled Ireland.

OF MICE AND ME

On Mardi Gras I knock back a few oyster shots, which are raw oysters dunked in cocktail sauce and drowned in vodka. With enough cocktail sauce and vodka, I could eat snot — which is about the same as eating oysters.

I respect the forthright ways of Passover. It's the only holiday where food is *supposed* to be miserable. It features bitter herbs, a fruit-and-nut paste designed to represent brick mortar, parsley dipped in tears, and the Bread of Affliction. *Bon apétit.*

On Cinco de Mayo we celebrate Mexico's victory over France in the Battle of Puebla by eating nachos from Texas.

Hot dogs on the 4th of July taste good mostly because we bury them in cheese, sauerkraut, relish and mustard. You could probably leave out the hot dog and not miss it. Made of ground ears and lips and looking like wet toilet paper dyed gangrene pink, we know it's not really food, but at least it's better than a bun full of neck. Hot dogs would be gray, except we dye them with *cochineal,* a red powder made from crushed beetles boiled in ammonia. But hey, that's better than gray.

In my family, Chex Mix is served at every holiday. Chex Mix is mostly butter, Worcestershire sauce and seasoned salt. Seasoned salt is salt salted with salt. A salt lick has less salt than seasoned salt. Seasoned salt has more salt than salt.

Tastes evolve as we age. I used to beg my mom for Wonder Bread. Now I despise it. I used to gag over sauerkraut. Now my mouth waters at the thought. I almost thew up the first time I saw an oyster, and now I like them fresh and chilled. I used to make fun of my dad for liking all these nasty things. So as I grow more and more to look like my father, as I eat more and more like he did, I fear that someday, some Thanksgiving, I'm going to blurt out, "Hey guys — save me the neck!"

IN THE BAG

I ran home, peeled off my Halloween costume and tossed it aside. I leaned up against the heavy wooden door of my closet, and peered into my bag of bribery loot.

Gripping the paper bag by its string handles, I opened it wide and put my face deep inside, taking a long sniff.

The smell of Halloween.

My mother didn't stock a lot of candy around the house. With six kids it wasn't worth the bother. The first of us who got wind of it would eat it all and hide the evidence. I didn't much like red licorice, but I'd hog it all anyway just on principle, to keep my siblings from having it.

Mom wasn't against candy. If I bought it myself, she figured I was entitled to it. After school I'd head to Bob's Kwik-Shop with my friend Harold, and we'd blow all the money in our pockets on candy bars: big fat chewy ones, sometimes three or four. Usually I'd get a few classics — Snickers, Nestle's Crunch, Mr. Goodbar, Reese's (there were no "Pieces" back then, and the chocolate/peanut butter pie was way bigger than today). Other times we'd try something new. The Cherry Mash looked pretty good on the outside, but the inside looked like it had already been eaten.

I'm not that picky. In fact, I consider myself a food slut. To this day, goat cheese is the only food that I have physically wiped off my tongue. I had expected it to taste more like cheese and less like goat.

OF MICE AND ME

Tootsie Pops took a little thinking. A popular commercial of the day featured a wise owl extolling the virtues of licking your way to the chewy center. I began to feel guilty about crushing the Tootsie Pop between my molars, and always tried to suck my way into it. Leave it to me to create rules about candy. Perhaps once or twice I actually licked to the middle, only to discover a slobbery Tootsie Roll inside, which I could have just chosen in the first place.

We'd take our loot back to Harold's because both his parents worked and we'd have the house to ourselves. We'd eat all our candy while listening to his *Man of La Mancha* soundtrack. At the time, that seemed perfectly normal.

So after a few long, exultant breaths, I pulled my face out of the trick-or-treat bag and dumped thine holy contents onto the carpet.

There were a few eyebrow-raising standouts. I scored a Salted Nut Roll. A whole, regular-sized Hershey bar. Who were these people? What do they do for a living, that they can give this stuff away to strangers? Would they adopt me?

Then there were the obvious turds in the punch bowl. The apple: I appreciate what you're trying to say, but keep your lefty politics off my Halloween. Do you think I'm dressing up in disguise and shaking down my neighbors with threat of tricks because I want to do the right thing?

Necco Wafers: as near as I can tell, it's candy made from colored sidewalk chalk. You'd only give this to kids you hate, so it seems I've made enemies.

A religious tract: it's inevitable that someone takes this opportunity, hoping some eight-year-old kid will stop in the middle of his Pixie Stix and say, "My belly is full but my heart is empty, and I'm asking Jesus to come in." I was church-raised, but if I felt emptiness and I had a choice between a tiny Jesus cartoon book and a King Size Kit Kat, I know what I'd reach for. Substituting a kid's candy with a religious tract is the best way to make him hate God.

The sorting begins. The "individual size" candy bars go in the keeper pile, even though to me the big Hershey bar was individual-sized. Today, Halloween candy bars are about the size of a fingernail, and they're called "Party Size," which I might understand if they were made of Ecstasy. For a candy bar, it's the equivalent of getting a birthday cupcake.

In: Tootsie Rolls, chocolate bars, Kisses, Kandy Korn.

Out: Circus Peanuts, those spongy tan things that don't taste like a circus or a peanut. The hard candy wrapped in plain orange and brown wrappers. Peppermints. Candy necklaces.

Popcorn balls: I can't resist taking a big bite, but despite all the colors and sparkles they're still just a stale, gummy ball of Karo Corn Syrup. Toss to the Out Bag.

Just then my mom walked in. "It would be nice if you would share with your brothers and sisters," she said. "You're the only one young enough to trick-or-treat."

"I know, Mom, I was already going to," I said as I handed her the Out Bag. "They can have whatever they want from here." She smiled approvingly. I smiled too.

THE MASKED PRETENDER

I love Halloween because 1) I cling to childish things, 2) I get to dress funny, and 3) my house is filled with candy bars.

Hopefully, thanks to my many years of experience, this Halloween will go smoothly. Last year didn't. It went something like:

7:30 AM: Wake up.

9:30 AM: Wake up again. I'm late. *Shit!*

11:00 AM: Go outside to replace burned out porch light bulb. Drop new bulb from six-foot ladder. It was the last bulb in the box. Go to store for bulbs.

11:45 AM: Return from store. It's time for lunch. Discover I don't have anything to eat but pumpkins and candy bars. Go back to store.

1:00 PM: Carve pumpkins. Pop seeds into the oven to roast for a snack, even though they've never even once turned out any good.

1:30 PM: Set out trick-or-treat candy. Discover there are only six pieces left. Go back to store.

2:45 PM: Return to discover kitchen full of smoke. Pumpkin seeds are on fire. Put billowing, charred cookie sheet out on the back porch.

3:00 PM: Answer phone. It's next-door neighbor, who thinks my back door is on fire. "Didn't that happen last year too?" I tell him to shut up.

4:30 PM: Try on Beaker costume. Discover I can't see out of the mask. Walk head-on into edge of open bathroom door.

5:00 PM: Regain consciousness. Ponder the ceiling. Why am I on my back? Where am I? *Who* am I? Look down at myself and deduce that I am someone from Sesame Street.

5:30 PM: It is time for kids to come trick-or-treating, which means it is time for a shot of tequila. Tequila bottle has only three drops in it.

5:31 PM: Another trip to store interrupted by doorbell. "Trick or treat!" Hand out candy. Ask kids if any of them has tequila. One does. He won't share.

5:35 PM: Swearing, rush back to store, leaving peel-out marks on the driveway. Stop to apologize to neighbor for nearly running over his six-year-old. Promise to replace his flattened jack-o-lantern bucket.

6:00 PM: Candy handing-outing now fully underway. Seems like more kids than usual because knot on my forehead is giving me double-vision.

6:30 PM: Another shot of tequila. Double vision cancels itself out. Neighbor kids complain that I'm not scary enough. Pull off Beaker mask, revealing giant purple knotted head. They run screaming.

7:00 PM: Find original *Frankenstein* movie on TV. Pour another shot.

8:00 PM: Older kids start showing up at the door. They all have pathetic, last-minute costumes: football players and hobos. They hold open pillowcases optimistically. Decide to stop answering door and keep candy for myself, because, hey — at least *I* dressed up.

8:10 PM: Crash into bathroom door again. Not wearing mask. No more tequila.

8:15 PM: Head to Halloween party. Car honk reminds me to take off my Beaker mask. Discover I'm driving on the wrong side of the street. Finally I scared somebody.

1:30 AM: Happy. Exhausted. Wide awake with a sugar buzz.

7:30 AM: Wake up.

9:30 AM: Wake up again. *Shit!* Late.

9:40 AM: Look at self in mirror, naked and wet, belly bulging. Either I had too much candy and booze or I got knocked up overnight. With Halloween, you never know.

SAY IT WITH MEAT

At Christmastime we often show our love with a salami. I don't know how Hillshire Farms survives the rest of the year, but during the Christmas season business must be booming, as neatly packaged grassy nests with unrefrigerated salami and warm wet cheeses are exchanged, often multiple times.

How salami came to be a customary gift at Christmas has been forgotten, but I suppose it has something to do with the end of the year and having to get rid of all those leftover pig parts that have been piling up since we made 4th of July hot dogs. I've never heard of anyone giving his sweetheart a big Valentine's salami, even though that's some good symbolism.

On Halloween we offer chocolate to the undead. I've seen most of the classic horror movies, and monsters seek flesh, brains and blood — salami, basically. None are ever placated with a peanut-butter cup. The closest I've seen was in *War of The Worlds*, when the alien first peeks out of its meteor-ship. Pastor Collins, who to non-Earthly eyes is dressed quite like an adult-sized Dove Bar, raises a friendly hand and says "We come in—" and gets zapped into sparkly dust before he can say "—peace." So much for the placating powers of chocolate.

But while chocolate may not work for fending off monsters, I think it would be a big improvement for Sunday Communion.

OF MICE AND ME

The celebration of Communion varies greatly from church to church. At my church they baked fresh bread and passed it around. It symbolized the body of Christ, which in this case was still warm. You tore off a chunk as it went by, and chased it with a sip of wine. I once visited a church down the street and was startled when the pastor laid a thin, dry wafer on my tongue that was as tasty as parchment. He said, "Peace be with you," and I was supposed to respond, "And also with you," but it came out "ack-ack-ack," because the wafer glued itself to my tongue. I couldn't stop myself from imagining it was the peeled sunburn of Christ. The pastor instructed me to keep my tongue sticking out for a moment, which was fine with me.

Why can't they at least use Nilla wafers? Or little cheddar-flavored crackers shaped like Our Savior. Jeez-Its? Better yet, offer little chocolate Jesuses — I'd be happy to line up for that, or for chocolates shaped like crosses or fish — any of the popular logos. God is good, and should taste like it. Communion chocolate would pair naturally with the wine, and as I said, we're already handing out bite-size Snickers to the rest of the risen dead.

At Easter, we celebrate the fertility season by biting the head off a chocolate rabbit.

For Passover we eat bitter herbs, just to remind ourselves how bad food can get, like Manischewitz.

To the Jewish, food must be *kosher.* To Muslims it must be *halal,* which is to say that it must be acceptable to God. In neither religion will God accept a salami.

During Ramadan, the power of food is symbolized by its absence, which is to say you don't get any. One of the benefits of a thirty-day fast is that, when you end it, everything tastes great.

Thanksgiving is the only holiday where food makes any symbolic sense. We celebrate being big, fat, rich Americans by eating big, fat rich American food. As Halloween zombies would say, that's a no-brainer.

Fourth of July is second only to Halloween in the weird use of sweets, as we toe up to the curb to admire a colorful parade of clumsy firetrucks and tanks while encouraging our confused children to leap into the oncoming traffic in pursuit of cheap candy thrown by strangers.

New Year's Day is a perfect opportunity for symbols of new life. We should eat eggs and oysters and enjoy the arousing qualities of chocolate. Heck, I suppose a salami would work too. Instead, we start our new year eating aspirin and going on a diet.

But making sense isn't always better. Last year I bought four bags of Halloween candy and only half made it out the front door, thanks to my quality control sampling. If it had been a big bowl of Halloween brains in my fridge, I wouldn't have been tempted to cheat.

FIRE IN THE FIREPLACE

Fire in the fireplace
   Full of Christmas cheer!
   Fire in the fireplace
Happy New Year!

Fire in the fireplace
Pretty as — *fuck!*
That's not the fireplace!
Call the fire truck!

MICHAEL B. CAMPBELL

ABOUT THE AUTHOR

Michael B. Campbell is an essayist and songwriter. His "Dumpster" essays close every issue of *Food & Spirits* magazine. His first collection of humor essays, *Are You Going To Eat That?*, was published in 2009, and his latest album of thirteen original songs, *My Turn Now*, was released in 2015.

Michael is good at all these things but one:[35]

- a) juggling Indian pins
- b) making pasta Bolognese
- c) folding a fitted sheet
- d) riding a unicycle

Get more Michael at

michaelcampbellsongwriter.com

mcwritingessays.blogspot.com

---

35 Answer: C.

MICHAEL B. CAMPBELL

OF MICE AND ME

www.ingramcontent.com/pod-product-compliance
Lightning Source LLC
LaVergne TN
LVHW051728080426
835511LV00018B/2934